Harmony Rules

Gary Chak-Kei Butt is the third generation of his family to be a healer. He is a traditional Chinese doctor, using acupuncture, acupressure, herbal medicine and, of course, food to treat his patients.

Frena Bloomfield, author of *The Book of Chinese Beliefs*, is a writer and journalist. Although British, she has lived in Asia for ten years. She has recently completed holistic health studies in the US and is a Natural Health Educator.

Also in Arrow by Frena Bloomfield

THE BOOK OF CHINESE BELIEFS

Harmony Rules

Gary Butt and
Frena Bloomfield

ARROW BOOKS

Cover calligraphy by Wong Ping Shu

Arrow Books Limited
17-21 Conway Street, London W1P 6JD

An imprint of the Hutchinson Publishing Group

London Melbourne Sydney Auckland
Johannesburg and agencies throughout
the world

First published 1985

Set in VIP Bembo by
D. P. Media Limited, Hitchin, Hertfordshire

Printed and bound in Great Britain by
Anchor Brendon Limited, Tiptree, Essex

ISBN 0 09 936840 4

This book is dedicated by Gary Chak-kei Butt
to his beloved mother and first teacher,
Mok Yue Tak

and by Frena Bloomfield to her two mothers,
Ena Gray Davidson Bloomfield and
Margaret May Davidson

Gary Butt's acupuncture teachers are: Leung Kok Yuen, Yim Kwan Hang, Lee Tin Yuen, Tse Wing Kwong, Choy Ma Kai, On Sai Chiu, Wong Ah Kwok. His herbal medicine teachers are: Lee Tin Yuen, Chen Chan Yuen, Tse Wing Kwong, Kwan Pak Chueng, Cheung Kung Yuan, Wong Ah Kwok.

Contents

Introduction

There is a great deal of interest these days in the healing traditions of the Chinese and there cannot, for example, be many people who have not heard of acupuncture even if they are somewhat hazy about what it is and how it works. Part of the new interest has undoubtedly been triggered by the opening of China which has allowed visitors to go in great numbers to that once-mysterious country and see for themselves what daily life is like. Most visitors are taken at least once to a clinic or hospital to see how the Chinese combine their traditional medical practices with the most modern Western medical treatments. This often comes as a surprise to Westerners who imagine that one but not both could be used, but to the pragmatic Chinese the point is to use whatever cures. In this way they are still extending a system of healing which has already been a matter of documentation and record for well over 2000 years.

A further boost to interest in Chinese medicine is the spread of what many call alternative medicine, but which we prefer to call complementary healing, in the last few years. Virtually every big city now has its acupuncturists, naturopaths, chiropractors, homeopathists, herbalists and a whole range of other healers offering the extremely wide range of healing now available in the West. This may be partly due to the course that Western medicine is taking, but is also due to the fact that many more people are becoming better educated in health matters and want to take personal responsibility for their good health. We can see this amply demonstrated in the increasing number of health-food stores everywhere and in the great numbers of people who have taken up physical pursuits to increase their fitness.

Therefore we feel this is an ideal time to introduce the subject of the most important part of Chinese healing – food therapy. It is true that most people think of Chinese medicine as acupuncture and herbs, but in fact the essential part of Chinese healing is prevention. It is not a system built around sickness and its symptoms – it is built around the maintenance of good health, and the heart of good health is good eating.

We have outlined in this book the basic system of food therapy as practised by the Chinese through 3000 years of careful observation. However, we have taken particular pains to ensure that it can be applied to the typical Western diet. It is not our intention to cater for those who are only stimulated by the exotic. We have made this a practical guide to good eating for everyone who lives in the West, as we feel that it is very important for the individual to understand how to attain and maintain good health by what he eats. It is the rare individual who can completely change his diet and we want this to be useful for the greatest number of people. Therefore almost all the food and drink classified here is well within the normal range easily available in the West.

We have explained how each food affects the body and which particular body organs it relates to, as well as including a list of common symptoms and conditions and the foods which affect them. At the end you will find a chapter containing recipe suggestions to strengthen particular body organs. We must point out that none of the foods work like modern drugs – they are not like shells which blast out both the condition and scatter side effects like shrapnel. Instead, they work the Chinese way – slowly, safely and harmoniously. If you have a particular condition you wish to treat – for example, hypertension – persist steadily with the various foods suggested over two or three months and then maintain your use of the foods which bring balance back to your body.

Meanwhile, you may like to ponder the words of Chief Minister Ch'i Po to the Yellow Emperor:

> Tao is the way of harmonious living which was practised by the sages and admired by ordinary men. Those who follow the rules of Yin and Yang will live, while those who go against them will die. Wise followers live in harmony, while the rebels live in disorder. To offend the laws of nature brings disharmony and causes the internal organs of the human body to malfunction.
>
> Therefore, the sages advised people to seek prevention rather than cure, to take precautions against chaos. This is the whole idea of harmonious living. To take medicine only when you are sick is like digging a well only when you are thirsty – is it not already too late?

Part One

The Development of Chinese Medicine

In the West we take things apart to find out how they work, but the Chinese have always done the opposite. They look at the whole and try to understand it in its entirety, believing that its nature is changed by pulling it apart or reducing it to its smallest unit. There are advantages to each way of looking at the world and nowhere is this more apparent than in a comparison of the Western and Chinese medical systems. Chinese medicine is based upon the study of man in harmonious relationship with himself – in mind, body and spirit – and with the universe around him, while Western medicine is based upon the study of diseases, their symptoms and treatment. The traditional Chinese medical practitioner sees as his ideal the prevention of sickness and the maintenance of harmony and, in fact, back in imperial times the court physician did not receive his wages if the emperor fell sick, since that was considered evidence enough that he had not been doing his job properly. The Western doctor aims to clear up the disease or damage with which he is confronted and will deal mainly with the part of the body which manifests the state of unhealth. The Chinese traditional doctor never treats only a part of the body, since it is inconceivable to him that a symptom can be considered by itself – he always looks for the whole picture.

There is no doubt that the symptom-oriented

system of Western medicine has in many dramatic ways outstripped the traditional medical practice of virtually every other part of the world. Excellence in treating bacterial, infectious and contagious conditions is the direct result of stripping elements down to their tiniest part, while the surgical miracles performed daily are due to the centuries of dissection of bodies and experimental explorations carried out on animals – both of which have been unacceptable to the Chinese in the past. Due to historical bans on the dissection of the human body, even now Chinese medicine is by Western standards somewhat vague about anatomy in certain ways.

However, we do find in the West now an increasing uneasiness about the current state of medicine. Treatments which are dire and invasive have brought about a frightening rise in iatrogenic conditions – illnesses caused by doctors and their treatment. Medical statistics from the USA indicate that a startling 45 per cent of all illnesses are iatrogenic. Many patients feel that they have become secondary to their ailments and that far too little attention is being paid to the person who carries them into the doctor's surgery, and there is a growing revolt against treatments which seem worse than the conditions they are supposed to alleviate or cure. The indifference of the machine is replacing human care and attention and the patient is finding that his family and friends are kept away at the very times when he most needs them to be near, when he is sick, in pain or dying. Doctors are no longer the magician-priests who bring care and cure to those who need it – instead they are becoming the technologists who monitor the machines with which the sick are now surrounded.

In Chinese medicine, however, there is a basic and enduring acknowledgement of the patient as a human being and an individual. Certainly the doctor will look at his symptoms but he will also take into account what manner of person the patient is before he defines his methods of treatment. There is no treatment for a symptom alone, only for a symptom which is part of a whole syndrome in a particular human setting. The Chinese doctor would consider it absurd, for example, that a whole group of dissimilar people be put on the same diet only because they shared the same disease. Whichever treatment the Chinese doctor chooses for his patient, it will certainly not be invasive nor will it have undesirable side effects, but the counter of this is that it is likely to take longer to restore full harmony to the patient. Chinese medical treatment does not aim for the overnight miracle cure, for the doctor knows that anything which can strike down a symptom that quickly must also bring about disharmony elsewhere in the body. The great strength of Chinese medicine is its effectiveness in regulating the function of the organs of the body and its weakness is in treating infections and conditions requiring surgery. On the other hand, the Chinese doctor would say that on the whole, if harmony is maintained in the body, then the patient would not be likely to fall prey to disease or even be as likely to have accidents.

To be healthy, a human being needs fresh air, clean water, exercise, the right mental attitudes and – most important of all – good food. This book will explore thoroughly what the Chinese doctor means by good food and show how that knowledge can be used by the reader to enhance his health.

The Chinese consider eating to be of paramount importance. There is even a Cantonese saying: Eating is as important as the sky. Food is essential for life because it is transformed into fuel for the body, but there is far more to it than that. It is not merely fuel. It is a great source of pleasure. It forms the focus of nearly every social gathering. It unifies the people around the table in a way which eating Western style does not. Many observers have commented that the Chinese live to eat, rather than eat to live, and this may well be because of the centuries of famine which decimated the population of China. Whatever the reason, however, because of their passion for food the Chinese have for thousands of years been deeply absorbed in the whole world of food and eating. This has led to long observation of the effects that different kinds of food have upon different types of people and to a systemization of food almost unknown among any other people, apart perhaps from the Indians.

Over the centuries it was seen that certain people preferred certain kinds of food, and gradually it emerged that these preferences were often dictated by the kind of person the consumer was. It became apparent that it was often body type which caused food likes and dislikes, as if the very cells of the body were shaping the appetite and its reaction to foods. What the body disliked, it rejected by showing signs of sickness or allergies.

Most people can easily learn to become aware of what is good for them and what they should avoid.

It only takes time and the ability to be a little observant about how food affects the body, the mental states and even the state of the spirit. Surprisingly, many people today eat in total ignorance of whether their food is good for them or not. They simply do not bother to observe what is happening to them and, through living on the kind of food which is basically unsuitable for their body type, they set themselves up for sickness. Having the right diet is not, according to the Chinese, a matter of calories, it is very much a matter of picking the right diet for that particular body. An awareness of how to select the right kind of food has been developed in Chinese society after thousands of years of observation. Most Chinese absorb this knowledge from childhood as they are brought up by older people already familiar with the tradition. Thus, even at the most superficial level, they will pick the foods and drinks which supply what they need. Around a table in a Chinese restaurant the diners will choose different teas for their individual needs. The properties of the teas differ – some are cooling, some heating, some are good for the lungs, others an aid to digestion, and so on. Therefore, each diner will order the tea which best fits the needs of his body on that particular day. Another day is very likely to see a different choice made.

This kind of awareness of food and its effects is common to most Chinese and it is not hard for a non-Chinese to learn how it operates. Many Westerners simply do not give much thought to the food they eat unless it is fattening or causes allergic reactions. But ignorant eating is one of the biggest factors leading to illness and could easily be rectified. As far as the Chinese are concerned, food is not merely a matter of proteins, vitamins and calories. In fact, a meal could contain just the right amount of all three and yet be unsuitable for the real needs of the eater and do little for his physical welfare or mental state.

It sounds like a very modern concept, that you are what you eat, but the Chinese have been aware of that principle for a very long time and, fortunately for us, have been collecting written documentation for at least 3000 years, if not longer. The system which we write about is not a passing fad, nor is it a crank diet which has suddenly soared to prominence for a few months without sufficient testing. The Chinese are among the most numerous people on earth and Chinese cuisine is perhaps the most widely spread in the world. It is not mere coincidence that Chinese dishes all over the world share the same ingredients and the same cooking methods. It is because the Chinese have found that their system works. However, it is not necessary to eat Chinese food to make this system work. It is entirely possible to measure whatever kind of food you normally eat against this system and find the way to balance out your own preferred diet for maximum gains in health and mental harmony.

Before the first written theories of food and medicine, the Chinese already had legends about the history of eating. According to ancient tradition, before the history of China really began, there was a time when there were great legendary rulers about whom stories are told but with no real evidence to prove that they existed. One of these legendary rulers was the Emperor Shen Nung, also known as the Holy Farmer and credited with inventing the Chinese lunar calendar. One story about Shen Nung says that he was the first to taste and classify many different kinds of food. He tried, so it is told, one hundred species of herb, being poisoned on seventy different occasions while undertaking this heroic task.

Be that as it may, the earliest written records to be found on food were those contained in a text known as *The Yellow Emperor's Classic of Internal Medicine*, which is the world's oldest medical textbook. Its Chinese title is *Huang Ti Nei Ching*, often known as the *Nei Ching* for short. The Yellow Emperor was also a legendary ruler, the third of the five legendary rulers, traditionally given the reign 2697–2597 BC although no one has so far really proved his existence. The book that bears his name, however, has been dated by scholars whose latest consensus suggests that it was written around 1000 BC, but based on earlier records that may either have been lost or only passed down in oral form from teacher to student over the centuries. The book itself is not like any other medical text in the world. It is not a list of symptoms or diseases – although such matters are dealt with – but a philosophical dialogue on the nature of man and the universe. The discussion takes place between the Yellow Emperor and his Chief Minister Ch'i Po, in the form of a Socratic dialogue in which the emperor asks questions which Ch'i Po answers, in the course of which the whole nature of disease and health is elaborated thoroughly. Although this was written so long ago, the text is still regarded as essential for would-be doctors following the Chinese tradition today.

The *Nei Ching* was the first of many classical medical writings, most of which are still in use. This not only reflects the Chinese love of tradition, which is undoubtedly a factor, but it also indicates the basic accuracy of many of the premises expressed in those early texts and which are therefore still valid now. Unfortunately, the idiom of the language has often proved an insurmountable barrier for Western-educated physicians who therefore often do not look into the texts to explore the contents. Nevertheless, there is now a wealth of Chinese medical writing available in translation covering Chinese medical discoveries of the last 2000 years. We mention only a few of the major contributions.

The physician known as the Hippocrates of China was Chung-ching Chang (AD 142–220) who was called the Medical Sage and whose pupils came from all over China. His speciality was the study of fevers, and he was a renowned diagnostician who created careful guidelines for the care and treatment of chronic and acute diseases. He left behind him a medical text entitled *Attacked by Cold*, which is a study of influenza and the common cold, not – as often mistranslated – a study of typhoid. (The confusion arises over the similarity in the two characters for the conditions.)

Everyone knows that one of the first things a doctor is likely to do is to check his patient's pulse, but not many people realize that this was a practice originally instigated in China. The first Chinese doctor to write on the pulse and its significance was Shu-ho Wang (AD 210–285) and his work was entitled *The Principles of Pulse*. This method of reading the pulse was brought into Europe by Arabic doctors whose medical knowledge was at that time far in advance of that in Europe and who had learned some of the secrets of Chinese medicine through trade connections with the Chinese. This contact enabled them to obtain many of the medical texts then in existence in China. However, Western medicine has not developed the art of taking the pulse readings very far, while the Chinese doctor can diagnose the condition of the body very thoroughly from the pulse alone. In Chinese medicine, the doctor takes the pulse at three points on each wrist and each point reveals the condition of the major body organs. A good pulse diagnostician – and that is not something which is easy to be – can read the reports issued by the pulse on what is happening within the body.

The standard medical textbook on acupuncture, still used today, was written in the third century AD by Hwang-fu Mi (AD 215–286). Although the *Nei Ching* does contain extensive references to acupuncture, it enumerated only 132 meridian points, whereas Mi identified 365.

In those early centuries there were not the divisions between science, medicine, religion and philosophy that the West sees today, and medical texts were often a mixture of information which some people would see as being superstition, and established observable data. A prime example of this was Hung Ko's text, the *Nei P'ien*. Hung Ko was a Taoist and his book contains the sum total of everything known to the Chinese at that time in the related fields of science, religion and philosophy. Until then many of the teachings in his book had been secret, passed down orally from teacher to pupil. His text has health guidance, recipes for immortality, and a pharmacopoeia of useful medical remedies and he is thus regarded as one of the world's first pharmaceutical chemists. Like many in his time he was an alchemist and he explored the refining of mercury and other elements. His text was translated into English for the first time by the Massachusetts Institute of Technology, largely because of its scientific content, but the MIT translation is not complete and many of the more mystical areas of the manuscript remain untouched and unknown to English-language readers.

The fifth century AD saw another major step in Chinese medicine when a distinguished herbalist, Hung-ching Tao, collected together all the available data of his time into a work titled *Herbs as Studied by Shen Nung*. This was a reference to the legendary Emperor Shen Nung, who was said to have investigated herbal medicines in China's prehistory but who left no written texts, naturally enough. Tao's work was the first thorough classification of herbal lore to be made and became an invaluable work of reference for all who came after his time.

Another great physician was the seventh-century medical writer Sze-miao Sun (AD 590–682) who wrote the classic *The Thousand Ducat Prescriptions for Emergency*. The title is a reference to a gold coin of the time and basically it meant that the remedies were worth their weight in gold. Sun commented in this work that a human being must have a good knowledge of food since, without that, he could not hope to keep healthy. 'Those who are ignorant about food,' he wrote, 'cannot survive.'

Sun collected a great many existing prescriptions which were already in popular use and added many more which he devised from his own long experience of treating the sick. Among his treatments he suggested the use of seaweed for effective control of goitre – seaweed being full of iodine. He also treated night blindness with liver, beriberi with beans, and used a naturally occurring ephedrine to cure asthmatic attacks – all of which remedies are used by Western doctors today, although in synthetic form. Sun was adamant in his belief that the right food was the better way to treat illnesses, and he even included in his book a whole chapter on food types, listing 154 of them with their therapeutic uses.

His own pupil, Sin Mang, developed these ideas even further and published his own work entitled *Prescriptions for Tonics and Nourishment*, listing some 214 types of food and their medical applications. This was later rewritten by Sin Mang's faithful student, Tin Cheung, who called the by then greatly revised work *The Pharmacopoeia of Therapeutic Food* and produced a much more formalized and systematically arranged text.

From this time onwards there was a great cavalcade of medical explorers, each of whom added his own special knowledge to the growing body of published texts. There was the acupuncturist, Wei-i Wang (eleventh century) who published a book on the acupuncture points located throughout the body. There was the first paediatrician Yi Chien (AD 1035–1117) who wrote *Treatments for Children's Diseases*. The first scholar to devote his energy to the study of medical jurisprudence was Tze Sung (AD 1186–1249) whose *The Righting and Redressing of Wrongs* expounds the art of diagnosing the cause of death through post-mortem examinations. In this work he covered such matters as rigor mortis, blood groups and the art of detecting when murder most foul has been done. The gastritis specialist Tung-yuan Li (AD 1180–1251) commented that health was closely linked with nutrition and that particular diets would help to clear up or prevent certain diseases.

It is possible to continue with the list, but the main point is to establish for the Western reader that the Chinese have studied medical matters and human beings extensively for the last 3000 years and have recorded the results of those observations.

Back in 200 BC in the document known as *The Record of the Institutions of the Zhou Dynasty*, the writer talks of the medical and health officials who should be included in an ideal state, some of whom would be the imperial dieticians. The task of these officials would be to plan the diet of the imperial court so that the foods were in harmony with the seasons, were nutritionally good and in harmony with each other. Over a thousand years later, in AD 1260, the court physician of the Tang emperors, Sze-wei Fu, wrote *The Importance of Correct Food and Drink*, a textbook which outlined the therapeutic use of food and drink and even included the correct cooking style and presentation of the dishes. This is still a classic of the Chinese kitchen.

Modern Chinese give the same importance to the choice and preparation of food and most of them would try to treat their health firstly by taking the appropriate food, only consulting a doctor when this did not seem to work. Knowledge of the medicinal aspects of food is absorbed by the Chinese in the easiest way, in their mothers' and grandmothers' kitchens. Quite often they may not know much about the complex theories which underly this knowledge, any more than the Westerner with a headache understands the intricate interaction with the body's pain mechanism of the aspirin he takes.

However, even though the Chinese have a very different way of classifying food and its effects, nevertheless they achieve results which often land in exactly the same place as Western medical knowledge. For example, even before anyone in the West knew about vitamins, every Chinese household kept a stock of dried orange peel in the medicine cupboard for use against the common cold – and of course it is in the skin that the greatest amount of vitamin C is to be found. How did the Chinese know about this? The answer is that they did not know about vitamin C, but they did know that orange peel was an effective medicine against cold symptoms and this practicality is the strength of Chinese medicine. In the West we are often obsessed with the question of how or why, when the one question we should ask of medicine is: does it cure? Perhaps the second question we should ask is: does it cure harmoniously?

There are other examples of practical results from Chinese medicine being confirmed by Western-style scientific exploration. Back in the Ming dynasty, around the year 1630, the venereal disease specialist Shih-cheng Chen wrote *The Secret Prescriptions for the Treatment of Venereal Diseases* in which he recommended using arsenic, a very effective remedy. Goitres were still being treated by iodine-rich seaweeds in the seventh century AD. High blood pressure has always been treated by Chinese herbs rich in rutin, which has been synthesized in Western medicine as a drug to bring down blood pressure.

The white fungus has long been used in soups as a blood cleanser, and it is only in this century that Western scientists have established that it seems to reduce cholesterol in the bloodstream and therefore to keep heart attacks at bay. This was only discovered when Western doctors noticed a significantly low incidence of heart attacks in the areas of China and Taiwan where the fungus grows. This led to investigation of the curious phenomenon.

Even modern hormone therapy had its equivalent in Chinese medicine. The placentas of animals, for example, were used as stimulants and as treatment for lung, heart and nerve diseases, while the pancreas of the pig was used to treat diabetes, known as the 'thirst disease' in the Chinese medical dictionary.

We give these examples merely to help Westerners unfamiliar with Chinese medicine to understand how it has often reached the same conclusions as Western medicine when it comes to effective treatment, even though it travels via a different culture, vocabulary and philosophy. It still meets in basically the same body with the same ailments and its aim is the same – to relieve suffering.

There are now extensive explorations of Chinese medicine, both in China, where Western and traditional Chinese medicine flourish, and in special academic situations. The Chinese University in Hong Kong, for example, is running an investigation into the effectiveness of Chinese medicine according to Western scientific method. This project is funded by the World Health Organization as part of its belated recognition that indigenous medical systems have many merits that have until now too seldom been explored, due to the dominance of Western medicine and the fear that it would seem superstitious or unscientific to assume any basis for the effectiveness of ethnic medical practice. Of the 700 or so main herbs used in Chinese medicine, some 100 have been found to be effective in the ways claimed for them by tradition. The rest remain to be explored by Western scientific means.

One drawback to such exploration in the past is that the traditional Chinese doctor would never have denied one patient treatment considered to be curative simply to make him a control against another patient who was receiving such treatment already. This is regarded as ethically wrong. Add to that attitude the fact that the Chinese have already been observing the effects of treatment for many centuries and noting down the results, and it can be understood why so many Chinese doctors do not feel it necessary to seek a Western-style apologia for their ways of treating medical conditions. This applies even more to studies of food, the passion of the Chinese. In the West, nutrition is not a required part of medical training and many doctors leave medical school with only the vaguest ideas about nutrition, although this does not always prevent them from having opinions about it. In China the study of food and its effects is central to medical training and an essential part of healing and health maintenance.

In this book we are seeking to impart as much of that knowledge of food as would be helpful to the reader wanting to take charge of his own well-being and even for the reader seeking nutritional help to control or overcome a symptom or condition which troubles him. We explain what effect food has on the body and tell you how the Chinese treat particular conditions. If you only want to know how you can make the system work for you, turn to the chapters on food and on ailments and symptoms. If, however, you also want to understand what Chinese healing is all about, you should also read the first few chapters.

Remember that above all else the Chinese respect facts and detailed observation, so you are encouraged to observe the effects of food on yourself. You know your body best of all and you can trust your own judgement, so feel free to try the various different foods and to shape your diet so that you can control your own health. It does not matter whether you believe this works or not. If you believe but do nothing, you are in as bad a position as the person who thinks all this is nonsense. So we encourage you to try our system and see if it works for you and whether it helps you to bring your own health up towards its most harmonious.

The Basics of Chinese Medicine

This chapter is written as an introduction to the central concepts of Chinese medicine, including the causes of disease and the special vocabulary of the Chinese doctor. Many people find the biggest stumbling block to understanding Chinese medicine is the way in which it is explained by the Chinese. The actual vocabulary and basic concepts sound esoteric at best and deliberately obscure at worst, but it is worth looking at why this is so. At its most simple, the reason that the terms used in Chinese medicine sound so utterly foreign is due to the language differences between English and Chinese. Many of these concepts are commonly used in everyday Chinese when people talk about their health – they do actually say that they are suffering from hot air in the lungs which causes their cough and they do decide to eat a cooling food because they are feeling over-heated.

There are, however, other complications. Since it is in the Chinese tradition to add to knowledge in the same idiom as in the original, Chinese medical writers are still using the language of 2000 years ago when it comes to expressing medical ideas. This seems very difficult to Westerners but is acceptable to the Chinese who are by nature and long training great preservers of tradition. Once Taoism became philosophically dominant, it also caused yet another overlay to be painted on to an already complex medical tradition and the result of all this is what we see today in Chinese medicine.

Our own aim is not to produce more traditional Chinese doctors, but to spread knowledge, so we have tried to find a good middle way through all this. We have explained the concepts as clearly as possible and have retained the specialized vocabulary only where strictly necessary and only after explaining it first. Many of the terms used in Chinese medicine are an expression of man's original closeness to nature and the Chinese doctor still considers that we are in fact very much affected by natural phenomena, but that most of us have become unaware of it. Part of our purpose in writing this chapter is to re-awaken such awareness since human beings who feel themselves to be part of the whole universe do not act destructively towards themselves or others.

The Causes of Disease

The Chinese have an entirely different approach to the philosophy of disease from that of most Westerners. This is partly because traditional medical practitioners had no awareness of the existence of germs, viruses and bacteria, but even today most Chinese doctors do not regard these as being the prime causes of disease. After all, they argue, twenty people may be exposed to a particular germ and yet only eight of them will become sick. Therefore it is obvious that there are other more important factors than infection which bring about illness. Interestingly, this is a view becoming much more prevalent in the West now, although good doctors have always been aware that an individual's state of well-being was affected by personal issues.

Some exciting new theories of illness are being considered now in the West, giving rise to the personality theory of disease. Western doctors talk of the 'cancer personality', the person who stifles anger and resentment until it becomes literally the disease which eats away inside them. There are the newly fashionable Type A/Type B personalities – the Type A a hard-driving over-achiever who pushes himself inexorably towards a coronary thrombosis, while more easy-going Type B takes life more wisely and teaches himself to play contentedly as well as to work. There is even typing according to blood group – the Type O Positive who can eat any kind of food and digest it well, thanks to their powerfully neutralizing body type which can cope with anything, while the Type B people have to be very careful about what they eat, since they often suffer from food sensitivities.

Therefore, although Chinese traditional practitioners do now know about germs, viruses and bacteria, these new discoveries have not in any significant way modified their basic approach to healing. Neither has it changed their ideas about what causes illness. Actually, to use the word 'cause' is a little misleading. The Chinese do not really look at any form of knowledge in terms of cause and effect, since this linear way of thinking is essentially Western. Instead, they look at the whole situation and observe its progress. From this, after a sufficient period of observation, they can create a picture of the natural course of events. Certain factors regularly precede particular states of disharmony and this is what allows disease to arise. Even our own word disease is a reference to the same basic idea. Dis-ease has much the same meaning as disharmony. What Westerners think of as causes are merely – to the Chinese doctor – the factors which precede disease. For the Western reader, however, it is more simple to list these factors as causes and it has the added value of creating an awareness of situations which may lead to disharmony – sickness – if the person concerned does not try to adjust them.

The Chinese classify the causes of disease under three headings – external, internal and miscellaneous. The external causes of disease are environmental factors, the internal causes are emotional factors and miscellaneous includes all those causes which can be considered neither external nor internal.

External Causes

The external causes are environmental ones, classified as wind, cold, heat, damp and dryness. These are regarded as causes for two reasons. One is the practical result of centuries of observation of natural phenomena and how they affect mankind, something which has been somewhat neglected in the West. People who are aware of how they are affected by nature are often those who have conditions which manifest when the weather changes – the rheumatism sufferer who knows by aching bones that it is soon going to rain, the migraine sufferer who has an attack when thundery weather is around, the allergic person who dreads the blossoming of flowers in spring and summer because of hay fever. Otherwise, we tend in the West to be quite unaware of how we are affected by climate and weather, largely because we live out of the reach of nature. Yet the natural environment still has its effect, though we are not trained to notice it. In fact, researchers in the West are now starting to look once more at the physiological effects of seasonal and climatic changes and we may find that those ancient Chinese healers were not far off the track in their observations.

The second reason why natural environmental factors are considered to be so important is that they reflect the Chinese belief that man is part of nature. He is not separate from it or above it. He is as much part of it as a tree or a river and therefore must logically be affected by natural seasonal and climatic changes in the same way. This may sound unlikely, but if you begin to observe these factors for yourself you may well find another picture emerging. It is certainly easy enough to test. Just start to be aware of weather and your own state of health and you will see if a correlation begins to show or not. The good thing about Chinese medicine is that you do not have to take anything on faith. Just watch carefully and decide for yourself.

Too much heat, too great a wind, and the human body becomes imbalanced as it tries to adjust to extreme conditions; unalleviated, this leads to sickness. We shall explain these concepts in more detail later in this chapter, so that the reader can apply them to understanding how his own lifestyle affects his health, but it is worth pointing out an important language difference between English and Chinese. The Chinese written language is not easy to translate adequately because of its complex nature. Each Chinese character contains within it a number of related ideas and concepts which are immediately apparent to the educated reader. Although an English word can trigger a number of ideas at once, this is more by cultural understanding than because of the actual word itself. In Chinese, the ideas and references are built into the actual physical form of the character, the strokes themselves. Therefore, when the Chinese use terms like 'wind' and 'damp' to describe illness and the cause of illness, they include a complexity of related ideas which the Chinese reader understands from the pictograph chosen to represent the term. We cannot do the same in English, since our language does not contain that possibility, so we shall explain all these terms at greater length further on, so that all readers who are interested can get a more thorough idea of what the Chinese doctor means by the terms he uses.

Now we shall take a closer look at the external causes of disease and explain the terms used by the traditional Chinese doctor more thoroughly.

Wind

Since Chinese written characters contain so many shades of meaning in their basic structure, it will be useful for the Westerner to remember that all the terms cited as external causes of disease are both literal and metaphorical. Therefore, when a

Chinese doctor describes an ailment as being due to wind, he is both referring to the climatic conditions of wind and also to the way in which that particular illness manifests in the body – i.e., as sudden eruptions of movement in the body, in the form of darting pains and so on.

In their literal form, the effects of wind are quite apparent even to a fairly inattentive observer. When there is a wind blowing, most living creatures are affected by it, including man. A high wind makes animals restless as any cat-owner knows. One way in which wind changes the environment is by altering the temperature and another is through what it carries with it – pollen, dust, pollution, particles, germs, viruses and bacteria. The wind direction is also significant. In southern China, for example, the wind which most affects people in their daily lives is the east wind. This is a rough, unpleasant wind which is mainly associated with spring, although it can appear in any season of the year. It makes people restless and uncomfortable, and is often associated with headaches, bodily aches and pains, influenza, the common cold and diarrhoea. It causes animals to hide away and brings despair to the hearts of fishermen, since fish are most reluctant to rise when the east wind is blowing.

It should not be very surprising that wind has this capacity to influence living creatures, since it is already widely accepted that there are some winds famous for their disruptiveness. Among them is the notorious Föhn wind in Austria, a warm spring wind which brings murder and mayhem in its wake, so drastic is the effect of the sudden temperature change upon the winter-accustomed

Austrians. Similarly powerful are the Khamsin, the desert wind of Egypt, the Sirocco of southern Spain and the Mistral in France. These winds have become famed merely because of the extremity of the changes they bring. The Chinese have developed a more subtle awareness of what weather does to health. Any reader can begin to observe for himself whether or not his state of being changes mentally and physiologically as the weather changes, and make his own decisions about the matter.

In terms of symptoms or disease, wind in the body is associated with severe conditions which suddenly arise and equally suddenly subside, although perhaps leaving a residue of change behind them. Typical wind afflictions are headaches – which are often brought about by atmospheric changes of which the person is unaware – strokes, tremors, convulsions and muscle cramps. Wind is also associated with allergies and with itching skin, mainly because of the particles carried in the wind which cause such reactions – pollen causing hay fever, pollution causing skin problems.

Cold

This is a concept which presents little difficulty to Westerners because we have more awareness of the effects of cold. As we know, cold can affect the whole body, even to the extent of lowering body functions and causing death. The obvious signs of extreme cold are a lowered temperature, slow circulation of the blood, cold hands and feet, pale face, absence of sweating, aches and pains in the body, muscular contractions, slow pulse and numbness in the fingers and toes.

Because the whole circulatory system is slowed down, body cells do not receive their required quota of blood and oxygen and, in terms of Chinese medicine, *chi* energy is blocked and the meridians affected.

Typical disharmonies resulting from an excess of cold are influenza, aches and pains in head and body, diarrhoea, nausea and indigestion. The disharmony brought about by exposure to cold lowers resistance. Controlled experiments investigating this have caused researchers to deny this connection, but the essential difference between those unwillingly caught in cold-exposure circumstances and those voluntarily taking part in experiments is their state of mind – a vital difference ignored by researchers.

Heat

This is usually associated with summer, as far as climate goes, but heat excess can appear in the body during any season of the year. Its signs are all fairly obvious – high temperature, fever, dry mouth, dry tongue, dry lips, thirst and a pressing desire for cold drinks, sweating, red skin and restlessness. A person suffering from heat excess is also likely to be irritable and, if in bed, will restlessly move about and stretch his arms and legs to try to find a comfortable position. Other heat signs are bleeding from the nose and gums, red eyes and a strong fast pulse. The patient may be delirious as well.

The person suffering heat excess is likely to have constipation and dark yellow or cloudy urine, while his tongue will be coated with a thick yellow film.

The over-heated personality shows hysteria and neurosis and people who eat too much heating food – sugar, many kinds of alcohol, spices, high animal-fat products – will find that their bodies try to deal with the heat excess by producing skin eruptions. The blood discharges such heat through boils, acnes, pimples and carbuncles.

Usually heat excess manifests suddenly and violently.

Dampness

Dampness is also often referred to as humidity, under which term it might be more easily understood by Westerners. Humidity affects many material things – books, clothes, leather, even electronic instruments – and, say the Chinese, it affects the human body no less. In fact, those who live in humid climates can easily observe the difference in the way they feel on a high-humidity day and a low one. Excess humidity enters the body and brings about physiological changes by upsetting the fluid balance and causing retention of fluid in the body.

People suffering humidity in the body feel heavy, tired and full of dull aches and pains due to the congestion throughout the system. Other signs are shortness of breath and tightness in the chest, nausea, vomiting, excess sputum and mucus, chronic diarrhoea and a wide variety of skin problems. Those who suffer arthritis or even who have had broken bones can often foretell the coming of rain by aches and pains in their bodies. This is because the humidity is already rising before the rain actually arrives and it causes blockages in the body *chi* which manifest as pain.

Problems of dampness usually take a long time to resolve.

Dryness

This is a condition which usually precedes heat, and a person suffering from dryness will have a dry mouth and lips, feel thirsty, have a cough with no sputum, dry skin, pass only a small amount of urine, have constipation, dry eyes and itching skin. He will feel restless and irritable and also sluggish.

It is often brought on by dry weather, which leads to coughing and chest infections in many people, due to lack of moisture in the air. The dryness causes an imbalance in the system which upsets body harmony.

Foul Air

There are two categories of foul air which lead to disease – natural and artificial. The natural occurrence of bad air comes about through a sudden imbalance of nature, such as when a cold front suddenly arrives or even when a sun spot occurs.

The Chinese were able to observe the effects of nature upon the body because they lived much more closely with nature than it is now possible for most Westerners to do, or – for that matter – for most Chinese these days. They formulated their theories of illness or disharmony at a time when real and intimate involvement with nature existed and when they had nothing clouding their perception of how nature affected human beings. It is hard for Westerners now to see very easily how the weather can affect them as much as the Chinese say it does. The easiest way to explore this is to keep a daily journal in which the weather and relevant climatic conditions are recorded together with personal health data. Then the reader can check for himself whether the theory is valid. This practice would be thoroughly acceptable to the ancient Chinese, who did precisely this in the first place, which is how they formulated the theories we record here. It will also increase awareness of how the really fit person must take into account the weather when considering his food needs if he wants a harmonious body.

In the West researchers are beginning to look at weather and human health and have come up with some intriguing discoveries. Hungarian researcher Kerdo Istvan has found that people breathe differently in summer and winter, their maximum rate of breathing being in January and February, their minimum at the height of summer in July and August. He also found that haemoglobin is at its highest in the summer and its lowest in the winter, while the spring is apparently the body's most vulnerable time. Other researchers have established that cold fronts cause an onset of neuralgia, mental illness and rheumatism, while most people are aware that every time the temperature rises or drops significantly there is an outbreak of influenza, colds and gastro-intestinal ailments.

To all of which the traditional Chinese doctor would just say with no surprise: 'Well, of course!'

The artificial causes of foul air are, alas, known to all who live in the modern world. They are industrial pollution, carbon monoxide, chemicals, radiation and other effluvia which has been pumped into the air. The air is one way in which the body is fed –

it feeds necessary oxygen and other elements to the blood. If that food is polluted, obviously the body becomes sick.

Those are the six major factors which bring about disease due to external conditions, but do not make the mistake of trying, from that information, to diagnose your own state of health only through considering the above syndromes of symptoms. No Chinese healer would do that. He would certainly take them seriously into account, but he would also look at many other factors – your appearance, your mental and emotional state, your physiology, pulse, skin and tongue – and ask you a lot of questions before creating a whole picture of who you are and where imbalances have come about.

However, through becoming familiar with the factors which can lead to that imbalance, the reader can begin to educate himself with regard to his health, since sickness is far down the road of disharmony and a sign that the person has not been aware soon enough of what was happening to him. He waited until he was thirsty before digging his well.

Internal Causes

The Emotions

A human being who is suffering emotionally in any way cannot ultimately be healthy, since emotional harmony is an essential element in health. There can be no separation of the feelings from the body, as if it were possible to have harmony in the one despite the lack of it in the other. Chinese doctors have always given full recognition to the part the emotions play in good health and consider the psychological state of the patient to be as important as his pulse or his physical appearance.

The earliest Chinese medical text, *The Yellow Emperor's Classic of Internal Medicine*, mentions the seven emotions that particularly affect the body – joy, anger, sadness, grief, anxiety, fear and fright. These days, most Chinese doctors would group these together as five emotions, since the difference between sadness and grief and fear and fright is mainly one of degree and possibly of duration of effect. When the practitioner speaks of the damage that these emotions do he is not really referring to one instance of them occurring suddenly and then passing, although in fact the Chinese ideal state of mind would be calmness and acceptance even in the face of extremity. But the real harm is done when a person is habitually subject to one of these emotional extremes. Then the balance of yin and yang is upset in the body and eventually actual physical damage can affect the functioning of the major body organs.

Joy

It may come as a surprise to the Westerner to find joy listed as a harmful emotion since we tend to think that happiness is a state desirable above all others. However, anything extreme brings its own disharmony, even joy. A certain amount of measured joy is a wonderful thing for the body – it improves the circulation of blood and energy and therefore tones up the system. Too much of it, however, damages the heart. Witness the case of the race-track winner who gets carried away in an ambulance instead of being able to go and pick up the winnings that caused his heart attack. As the Chinese doctor says, it is too much joy which brings sudden death, not sadness.

The heart which is damaged by too much joy can suffer palpitations and angina, while insomnia, irritability and dyspepsia can trouble the person who experiences the emotion. A typical example would be the lover looking forward to a meeting with his beloved. Rather than peace and serenity, he is more likely to feel uneasiness in the pit of his stomach, be unable to sleep, unwilling to eat and find it hard to concentrate on anything else. Most of the symptoms of being in love are disruptive ones which indicate disharmony in the mind and body and they are symptoms specifically associated in Chinese medicine with a heart over-loaded with excitement.

Anger

Anger is one of the most damaging emotions. It attacks the liver, which is the organ most susceptible to emotional disturbance – apart from the heart. It is also true that a mulfunctioning liver can give rise to anger, which is why we refer to irascible and brusque behaviour as 'liverish'. This can soon become a malignant cycle – anger giving rise to liver damage which in itself creates new anger. There is also a clear link between emotional frustration and the liver, which increases the anger that people feel when they consider themselves to be trapped in a situation.

Although the expression of anger is fashionably

considered to be healthy, the Chinese doctor would not agree. It is better for the health to do something that takes the mind off the anger until it has decreased, then to deal with the situation. To give outward expression to the anger in an extreme way hits the liver hard, which is why the body can feel physical effects from anger long after the outburst has taken place. In fact, the latest research in the USA into this question is beginning to come down on the side of moderation. Investigators found that, far from discharging anger by expressing it, people who habitually confronted others in an angry way felt more and more angry and created responding anger around them. This conforms with the theory of Chinese medicine that anger hurts the liver which in turn creates more anger.

People who habitually feel anger suffer liver diseases and disturbances of the liver, as well as pains in the ribs, muscular cramps, red eyes, abnormal menstruation, pains in the testes and hypertension.

Anxiety

Anxiety injures the spleen and the stomach and can produce disruptions in the eating pattern, as does any disharmony in the relation of these two organs. Therefore the over-anxious person could have an extremely poor appetite or might over-eat. This emerges in anorexics and binge eaters, both over-anxious types. It can also result in irregular bowel movements, fatigue, dizziness, palpitations, a poor memory and distension of the abdomen.

Grief

Grief includes the whole range of feelings which we

describe variously as sadness, misery, melancholia, depression and even just feeling blue. This range of emotions damages the lungs, partly because the person suffering from grief tends not to breathe properly. The breathing is usually shallow and superficial, starving the lungs of oxygen and leaving pockets of stale air down in the deepest parts of the lungs which then become prone to infection. The body does make attempts to rectify this – this is why sad people sigh a lot. It is the body's way of trying to get the much-needed air which is not being obtained through normal breathing.

Someone who is habitually sad is likely to develop a range of symptoms – coughing, asthma, dysponea, excess sweating, pains in the chest, numbness of the extremities, fatigue and a pale face. Because the breathing pattern of a depressed person deprives the body of oxygen, it can be said that sadness eventually pervades the whole body.

Fear

Fear attacks the kidneys, which is why sudden terror induces an urgent desire to urinate and also why novelists so often refer to their heroes' bowels melting when faced by fearful odds.

The sufferer from constant fear is likely to develop some of the following symptoms – palpitations, ringing in the ears, poor hearing, aches and pains in the joints, muscular tension, lower-back pain, impotence and a variety of mental disorders.

Twentieth-century diseases and their emotional causes

In order to give further examples of the effect of

emotions on the body, we look here at some of the commonest health problems of our time and their emotional aspects. This is not to say that all these diseases do not have organic and environmental causes too. Since Chinese medicine is holistic and considers the state of mind, body and spirit, none of the contributing factors would be ignored. However, it is worth pointing out the dangers of emotional habits which can lead to serious illness, if the sufferer does not make an attempt to restore harmony to the feelings. If the reader finds that some of these states describe his own, he would be well advised to consider seriously what he intends to do about it. Not all answers are contained within the individual, although finally all the efforts do have to be made by that individual. In the twentieth century we are fortunate to have many ways of looking for harmony within – through religion, through psychology and counselling, through many kinds of physical and mental disciplines and any of these can be the answer for a particular individual.

The major causes of death in developed countries are heart attacks, cardio-vascular accidents or strokes and cancer. Major debilitating but not fatal conditions are rheumatism and digestive troubles. A new problem which has recently joined the list of common conditions with life-affecting dimensions is sexual in origin – impotence or sheer disinclination towards sexual activity and frigidity or non-orgasmic capabilities in women. All of these diseases and conditions have clear emotional origins, as far as the Chinese doctor is concerned, although that may not necessarily be the prime cause.

Cardio-vascular conditions

These may originate in any of three major organs – the heart, liver and kidneys. If they originate in the heart, this denotes the typical executive type and his syndrome of affliction – continual stress and unrelieved tension. A certain amount of stress is necessary for the body to function well, but all too often these days the stress is of a negative kind. It keeps adrenaline flowing to the extent that the heart is over-excited. The original function of stress was to get the body ready for action. To maintain stress over weeks, months and years in the form of daily battles through crowds, against business colleagues, against an increasingly uncalming environment is dangerous. Worse still, many of the kinds of exercises which stressed people are attracted to are in themselves stressful; exercise which emphasizes high adrenaline, competition and battle, while locking further tension even more deeply into the body – jogging, aerobics, squash, tennis. If this describes you, find a better way to deal with your stress, rather than wait for the heart attack which will disable you or the stroke which might rob you of your faculties, if not of your life. Remember that money is worth nothing if you are too brain-damaged to add it up, and whatever you attain in business will be lost if you are disabled by a heart attack.

If the liver is the site of the cardio-vascular accident, then this is anger at work. To be angry once in a while is not good for the liver but it will not do lasting damage, but if you are constantly losing your temper, flying off the handle, shouting and cursing other people, muttering angrily to yourself about small incidents, you are doing irreparable harm to your liver. Find another way to deal with your anger. Better still, get to the root of your anger – is it really everyday life or is it old anger that you have never confronted that keeps spilling over into your life now? Talking angrily to another person about your grievances will only create more anger in you. Instead, walk your anger off or read a book or do something to take your mind off it, then return to deal with the issues that made it arise and talk them over calmly, without giving way to rage. This is the harmonious way to deal with the situation.

Cardio-vascular accidents also have their origins in the kidneys. This comes about when a person is constantly anxious and insecure, fearful and full of doubts about himself. Fear depletes the kidneys and leads to hypertension.

The kind of person most likely to be involved in a cardio-vascular accident is an outgoing yang type, someone who can express what he feels but cannot easily discharge the effects of accumulated negative emotions. If this is you, beware.

Cancer

We are in the midst of a world epidemic of cancer right now, especially in developed countries where one in four deaths is due to cancer. There are many reasons why but we can bring them down to three major causes – environment, food and emotions. There can be no doubt that pollution is a major factor in cancer, as is the kind of food we eat and the enormous army of chemical additives which no other generation has had to deal with in the amounts we consume daily. But another very important underlying cause is emotional.

In temperament, cancer people differ from the cardio-vascular accident people. They are more likely to be yin people, introverted, inward-looking and concealing many of their feelings, holding on to emotions which quietly eat away at them and are not easily resolved or released.

Cancer of the liver, for example, is associated with suppressed anger. The kind of person who wages secret battles with other people but does not speak them out, the person who is often angry inside but conceals it, sometimes even from himself. If there is no sign of alcohol, hepatitis or food as a major cause, then look for the hidden anger which congests the liver and blocks its energies until they become completely inward and bring destruction to the healthy cells.

Lung cancer, when not due to industrial injuries or tobacco smoking, is a product of sadness. This is not the outward obvious sadness of the yang person. This is the quiet despair of the deeply pessimistic person who has no hopes for the future. As the Chinese doctor says, if you are sad, lung cancer will become your good friend.

Stomach cancer can be due to eating habits – pickled foods among the Japanese for example – or to already established disease like stomach ulcers or chronic gastric troubles. But it is also the product of worry and anxiety, an aspect of character in the person who yearns and longs for things he cannot ever have. This swallowed discontent becomes symbolized in cancer, something which the person cannot stomach any longer.

Gastro-intestinal problems

These also largely come from worries, especially in the person who has great expectations and great disappointments and cannot accept them.

Arthritis

There are a number of kinds of arthritis but they all originate from the kidneys. They are brought about through fear, constant nagging unsatisfied fear left unresolved because of the way in which it is repressed. This is not the hot angry fear which might find expression, it is the cold clinging fear which cannot easily be eradicated. This is why rheumatic attacks frequently coincide with a life crisis – it is fear which precipitates the attack. The Chinese medical theory explains the link between the kidneys and fear in the following way. They consider that the kidneys regulate bone growth. Therefore, anything which harms the kidneys leads to degeneration of the joints with consequent inflammation and infection – hence, arthritis.

Impotence and frigidity

While the Chinese doctor would largely attribute both these to depletion of kidney function through sexual excess, he would also look for an emotional factor and would expect to find fear as the underlying cause of sexual disfunction. We look at this in more depth in the miscellaneous causes of disease.

It would be possible to write a whole book merely about the effect of the emotions on health, but that would rather detract from the holistic aspect of Chinese medicine which looks at every possible factor – physical, emotional and spiritual –

to form a complete picture of what is happening in a particular individual. However there are some warning signals in the above and, if you find any of it especially relevant to yourself, it is time to do something about it. Just as Chinese medicine looks strictly at you as an individual – and never at you as a case or disease or symptom – so it also recognizes that there is only one person who can bring your life into harmony: You.

The Miscellaneous Causes of Disease

These are caused by mistakes in lifestyle which lead to imbalance and they are largely self-evident.

They include traumatic injuries such as broken bones, sprains, cuts, burns and scars which cause blockages in the natural circulation of blood and energy. This causes damage to cells and can give rise to a wide range of linked diseases.

Mental and physical exhaustion are very common among Westerners, who give themselves very few ways in which to carefully husband their energies in harmony. Even the ways in which they do choose to relax often do just the opposite. For example, many of the most popular forms of exercise, far from relaxing the body, only create further problems. Jogging is a prime example of this, as an exercise which is essentially disruptive of body harmony and physically damaging. People who feel good from jogging do so because of the addictive nature of the endomorphines produced by the brain, not because the exercise is doing good. Many people either work too hard or are tied to jobs which they feel are unsatisfying and unfulfilling and both these conditions produce continual feelings of exhaustion. This upsets the balance of yin and yang and makes it even more difficult for the individual to find peace. It also lowers the body's resistance to disease, since being physically ill is often the only way some people feel they can allow themselves to have time free from their work.

Lack of exercise is a notorious cause of illness. Without exercise of some kind – the right kind – the balance of the body cannot be maintained and circulation of blood and energy grow sluggish. This becomes a predisposition toward disease.

Also under the heading miscellaneous comes nervous and physical exhaustion through over-indulgence in sexual activity. This may not seem as obvious or even as acceptable as a cause of illness. However the Chinese believe that the kidneys store the energy which the body needs for growth and indeed for the continuance of life itself. This energy is known as kidney *chi* and, when used up, that is the end of life. Sexual activity uses up this kidney *chi* and therefore a reasonable balance should be observed in the sexual life. This condition also contains a psychological factor since it is very likely that a person who expends a great deal of energy on multiple sexual acts is not either getting or giving enough of the other essential parts of a relationship. Therefore it is very possible that the frequency of orgasm is not accompanied by feelings of fulfilment and this will rebound on the individual's mental health.

According to the great physician Sze-miao Sun, sexual intercourse resulting in ejaculation for the man and orgasm for the woman should take place with the following frequency:

from the ages of twenty to thirty, once in four days;
from thirty to forty, once in eight days;
from forty to fifty, once in sixteen days;
from fifty to sixty, once in twenty days;
from sixty to seventy, once a month;
over seventy, it is time to cease unless the body is very strong.

In fact, harmonious sexual intercourse is regarded as being a great source of good health and physical well-being which thoroughly accords with the yin-yang theory. After all, yin is female and yang is male, so heterosexual intercourse represents the ideal harmonizing of the universe.

These theories of sexuality did stray off the orthodox path occasionally in the course of Chinese history. There was a particular heretical sect of Taoist followers who formulated a different theory. They reasoned that a man could have intercourse as much as he liked as long as he did not ejaculate, but held back while the woman had her orgasm. Then he could have the benefit of her yin energy while retaining his own yang energy. A great deal of thought went into the techniques of withholding emission and instead reabsorbing the semen into the body system, drawing it upwards to the spine and finally to the crown of the head – which was supposed to lead to immortality. What it did lead to in actuality was the sexual abuse of young women or even girls, since it was felt that a virgin had particularly powerful yin energy. Even today there is a certain leaning among some older Chinese men towards very young girls, which is rationalized by the claim that they will retain their virility with this practice. It is regarded as an unhealthy obsession by Chinese doctors.

It is interesting to look at the AIDs phenomenon in the USA, and now elsewhere, in the light of Chinese views of sexuality. In terms of Chinese medicine, this fatal syndrome is thoroughly explicable. Almost without exception, those who have developed AIDs have taken part in highly promiscuous sexual activity over an extended period of time. According to the Chinese, sexual energy draws from the kidneys, but they also play a more important part even than that. It is in the kidneys that life *chi* is stored and each human being has only a finite amount of that. When it is used up, the person dies and it is this life *chi* which gives the body the strength to fight infections. When sexual energy is depleted by excess, the kidney *chi* in general is also depleted. This leads to a deficient immune system which can no longer fight invasion by germs and viruses.

An additional complication in the AIDs syndrome comes from the fact that the majority of victims are male homosexuals. In energy terms, male homosexual intercourse creates an extreme yang situation, as opposed to the ying-yang exchange of heterosexual intercourse. This yang imbalance is partly due to a reaction created in the male by the presence of sperm from another male, which cannot be assimilated into the body system without creating excess yang conditions. All the diseases particularly associated with AIDs – the cancer, the skin eruptions, the rare type of pneumonia – are extreme yang reactions. This cannot be balanced by the body and it cannot be treated successfully because the life *chi* itself has been depleted to such an extent that there is none left for the person to utilize, which is why all AIDs victims die.

The last, and perhaps most important, of all the miscellaneous causes of disease is wrong eating. There are general guidelines which every Chinese tries to follow when it comes to eating. He knows that he must stop eating when his stomach is 75 per cent full, to avoid over-taxing his digestive system. He does not ingest too much sugar, believing that this creates mucus throughout the system and has a far-reaching effect on health. This mucus is not only produced in the nose and throat where it causes catarrh and coughing. It is also found in various forms in the inner ears, stomach, lungs and blood vessels. In the blood vessels, it is cholesterol. In the lungs, it causes asthma attacks, in the stomach it leads to nausea and vomiting and in the blood vessels it brings about thrombosis. It also stresses the spleen and pancreas and is therefore related to diabetes.

In the same way, the Chinese avoid taking too much salt. Salt is recognized as a stimulant, which is why so many people are addicted to it, and it particularly affects the kidneys. Since the kidneys are linked with sexual energy, a highly sexed man is known as a 'salty man'. Even in the West we reflect the same thinking by calling sexually explicit humour 'salty'.

Sour-tasting foods and liquids are regarded as stimulating to the liver and gall bladder and they improve the secretion of bile, as well as having a slight dilating effect upon the vascular system.

However, an excess of such food and drink leads to imbalance and therefore eventually to ill health. For example, when dieters take to drinking large amounts of unsweetened grapefruit and lemon juice, they experience a certain weight loss which is actually due to the disruption of healthy interaction between liver, stomach and spleen. It is especially due to lack of harmony between the stomach and spleen, which are the two organs the Chinese mainly associate with the absorption of food and drink. The cost of pleasing weight loss will be a gradual loss of function in the major body organs, which will bring its own price later.

A certain amount of spicy food is also good for the body. It gives a boost to the lungs and the large intestine and aids excretion, as anyone can testify the morning after a rich dinner of hot spicy food. Spices include the obvious – pepper, chilli – but also garlic. In fact, anyone suffering constipation can clear his system by taking large amounts of garlic in his evening meal. Over-use of spice can have a limiting effect on the functions of the lungs and large intestine, bringing frequent attacks of either diarrhoea or constipation. Interestingly, this need not necessarily happen in a country where spicy food is the norm. This is because most societies have tended to build up the diet needed by their bodies, given their particular environment and physical type. In India, for example, the water is classified as cooling and therefore the spicy diet comes out of a natural inclination to balance the cooling water with hot food. Not all water can be classified as cooling. Some can be neutral, while in a place like Hawaii it is actually considered to be heating because of the high percentage of sulphur and other minerals in the water, due to the volcanic origins of the island.

Therefore, before you head for the curry pot you should be aware of whether you are basically a yang or yin type. If you are yin, you will do very well on even large amounts of spicy food, but if you are yang you should control your yearnings for stimulating foods or you may risk becoming excessively yang. An occasional outburst of curry fever will not do you too much harm, but you must be moderate in indulging that particular longing.

Visiting the Doctor – Chinese Style

When a person visits the Chinese traditional healer the doctor will examine him according to the classical recipe of his medical texts known as the Four Examinations. These consist of various ways of assessing the patient and will include the Visual, Listening and Smelling (expressed by the same verb in Chinese), Asking and Touching.

Visual

The doctor looks at the patient's general appearance, his behaviour and his psychological mien. He will notice the colour of his face, the condition of his tongue, eyes and hair. He will examine his nails, looking for their colour and structure and whether they are brittle or strong. He will examine any excretions or secretions relevant to his quest.

The general state of the patient becomes apparent through this visual examination and one of the most thorough parts will be examining his tongue. The Chinese have a highly developed system of reading the messages the tongue tells by the basic colour, shape and coating of it. Most Chinese doctors even have as part of their surgery equipment a tongue box – a set of twenty-six tongues modelled after the range of conditions likely to be seen in the normal course of medical duty.

Listening and Smelling

In this, the doctor is looking for indications which will show whether the patient is suffering from an excess or deficient condition. He listens to the voice – whether it is small and quiet or loud – to coughing, to the smell of his body, of his breath, urine and faeces, and relates all this to his condition.

Asking

This is an interrogation, the purpose of which is to form a complete patient history. The doctor will ask about behaviour patterns, whether the patient feels heat or cold, suffers pains in the body and what kind of pain, how he sleeps, his family and personal medical history, his diet, his psychological and emotional state.

Touching

Although this is the last of the four, it is perhaps the most important, and its central focus is the taking of the pulse. This bears very little relationship to the taking of the pulse in Western medicine. In feeling the pulse, the Chinese doctor obtains a wealth of information his Western colleagues can only obtain through a battery of tests. He feels three pulses on each wrist: on the left wrist the pulses represent the heart, liver and kidneys, while the right wrist pulses represent the lung, spleen and something known in Chinese medicine as the *min moon*, which is an energy reading for the centre point between the kidneys. This point in acupuncture is on the lumbar spine. It is known as the gate of life and a needle inserted deeply will kill the patient.

Medical texts galore have been written about the

pulses and different schools of thought about how many there are. Many Chinese doctors say that there are twenty-eight classic types of pulse, but Gary Butt follows a system which says there are actually only eight basic pulses and six kinds of characteristics, and the rest is merely adding further variations to those basics. The eight kinds of pulse are superficial, deep, slow, fast, smooth, uneven, excess and deficient, and the possible characteristics of these are that they may be tight, spongy, flooding, fine, weak or moderate. All of these can be felt by careful palpation of each pulse, and from such an examination the doctor can tell the condition of the various internal organs and whether there is anything wrong. If there is anything wrong, from palpation the doctor can tell whether this is a new, acute or chronic condition and how long the patient is likely to take to recover.

A good doctor can use only the visual and the pulse to make a diagnosis. In fact, during the Ching dynasty there was one famous physician nicknamed 'But Man Chan', which means 'Never ask questions'. He had a long thin consulting room with a desk far back from the door. It took a patient at least fifty paces to reach the doctor and, by the time he had walked that far, the doctor was already able to tell him what his condition was and what he must do about it.

Part Two

The Special Concepts of Chinese Medicine

In Part Two we explain some of the basic concepts of Chinese medicine which are peculiar to the Chinese. Many of them are probably already somewhat familiar to many readers because of the new and rising interest in other medical systems. Most people will have heard of yin and yang, for example, or of the meridian system of acupuncture, and we aim to introduce them more thoroughly in order to give the reader a sense of what lies at the root of Chinese medicine.

If some of the language seems odd, it must be remembered that this is a very old system with its own basic jargon, just as any system of specialized knowledge has a dialect of its own familiar to those who use it and often incomprehensible to those who do not. Our aim is to make the jargon of Chinese medicine familiar and to do that we can only introduce the ideas. For those who are already familiar with them, there are other much more complex texts available. Although some of the concepts may seem obscure to Western readers, it is worth remembering that most Chinese people will commonly use these terms to describe their own health or illness. It is, perhaps, just the metaphor of everyday medical life. In the West we have grown so used to our metaphors that we often do not recognize how odd they are. For example we speak of the illness known as influenza. This is the Spanish word for 'influence', so we commonly refer to a common condition with familiar symptoms as an 'influence' which has affected us. It remains from historical times when illness was constantly thought to be caused by influences, humours and vapours, but we use it specifically now. Many people still talk of children suffering from 'growing pains' even though there is no natural phenomenon associated with growth that should medically cause pain.

In the same way, many of the Chinese terms used are metaphors and expressions which strike ringingly on our ears because their very unfamiliarity makes us pause and consider them. A foreigner might ponder long and hard about what kind of influence we think causes influenza – whether it is a superstitious belief, whether it is actually an environmental factor or a climatic one – and we would think him strange to pause so long over our second most common affliction after the ordinary cold. The same is true of many Chinese medical expressions.

Yin and Yang

Understanding the theory of yin and yang is both easier and also more difficult than most Westerners think. The problem, if there is one, is of intellectual approach. In the West we think of the world in black and white terms and opposites, while the Chinese regard it against the background of their philosophical ideal, the balance of harmony. For the Chinese, yin and yang are not opposites – rather, they form together a harmonious whole and neither could exist without the other.

The other major aspect of yin and yang that is sometimes puzzling to Westerners is that they are never fixed and immutable. In fact they are changing all the time, but always in relationship to each other. Chinese philosophers of old knew that the universe and everything in it was constantly moving and changing. This is one of the basic tenets of the Chinese theory of the universe which has brought ancient Chinese thinking right in line with the newest and most radical theories in modern physics. This is also why modern theoretical physicists can use Chinese terminology for these exciting new approaches to the question of what the universe is and how it works. It is not merely a question of a matter of choosing a pleasing title that made Fritjof Capra name his book *The Tao of Physics*. It was also the realization that he, as a twentieth-century physicist, and the Chinese philosophers of

3000 years ago had a whole lot in common in their ideas.

We cannot really explain in a satisfactory way how the Chinese had that knowledge so long ago when we have only just come to that comprehension ourselves here in the West. Those ancient thinkers knew, it seems, that the universe was ever-growing and ever-changing, just as they knew that – despite any appearance to the contrary – at the innermost heart of the world was energy in constant motion. They knew that this apparently solid world was nothing of the kind and they understood it, despite having none of our sophisticated laboratory equipment to measure such phenomena or record it, and despite a lack of experimental approach to prove the matter one way or the other.

Even wanting to know how the Chinese knew what they did is very Western. The Chinese have always observed what is and recorded that. They have no real interest in why, or how, it is. Chinese medicine is a good example of this way of thinking. The considerable literature of medical matters concentrates upon what is – what is the human body, what is the course of diseases, what is the treatment for those states of disharmony. It does not on the whole approach the question of why – why does acupuncture do what it does and how do we know, why does this herb cure that condition, and so on. These are secondary matters.

For those interested in such secondary matters, there are some ancient Chinese legends which explain how knowledge came into their hands so early on. These stories tell of the coming to China of a strange race of people seven feet tall and clad in outlandish clothing. They were called the Sons of Reflected Light and arrived in about 10,000 BC. They bore with them knowledge far in advance of anything known by mankind at that point and they taught what they knew to the brightest and best from all over China. They taught medicine, science and philosophy, as well as a wide range of arts and crafts, and once they had taught all they could, they left again as mysteriously as they had come. It was their teachings which later formed the bulk of all Taoist knowledge.

The yin-yang theory pervades all Chinese thinking. Everything in the universe is either yin or yang – the world itself, the objects in the world, mankind, the parts of the body, the functions of those parts, the medical conditions which affect those functions. Neither yin nor yang is absolute. Even the most yin thing has a small element of yang within it and vice versa – that is why the symbol of the relationship of yin and yang looks as it does. That is to remind us that because yin and yang are always changing, yin can become yang and yang can become yin, according to the flux of the

Yin-Yang Symbol

universe. Nothing in this world is fixed and immutable.

Originally the written character for yin was a pictograph which meant 'the shady side of a hill' and the character for yang meant 'the sunny side of a hill'. However, the meaning has now become so extensive that it includes the whole universe and everything in it, defined as yin or yang. So, over the ages, the meaning of yin has extended and now the things which are considered to be yin include night, the moon, earth, winter, female, cold, passive, empty and so on. Yang applies to day, the sun, the sky, summer, male, hot, active, full and so on. For further examples of yin and yang, see the Yin–Yang tables on pages 71, 77 and 78.

The terms yin and yang are applied to Chinese medicine as well as to every other field of knowledge and activity. Thus certain parts of the body are yin and others yang and different medical conditions are either yin or yang, and can affect the body accordingly and even change its nature. Thus even a yin type of person could become quite yang under the influence of a yang disease. For example a yin person might typically be quiet, calm and softly spoken but, if he began to suffer from a yang liver condition, this might bring about significant changes in his behaviour. He could well start to show the irritable and angry characteristics commonly associated with yang liver conditions. This can also be brought about through diet quite deliberately. A yin person might choose to change his temperament through food, or the parents of a very yang child – a child suffering from excessive yang and showing this through temper, tantrums, shouting, hyperactive and destructive behaviour – might decide to cool the excessive yang by paying more attention to what their child eats and keeping him from dietary excess.

It might be of interest to the reader to know something about the way in which the Chinese classify the major organs of the body. Before embarking on a simplified explanation, however, it is worth pointing out that the Chinese sometimes mean something rather different by particular organs than the Westerner might assume. This is because, when they talk of the liver or the heart, they are really referring to the functions of the organ. The function is considered more important than the shape or the position or structure of the organ. In some ways there are no direct parallels between Western medicine and Chinese medicine and it can be confusing to try to find them.

Therefore in considering the nature of the body organs we shall also indicate what the Chinese think about their function and whether it is thought to be yin or yang.

Table 1 *Yin and Yang Organs*

yin	*yang*
Heart	Small intestine
Liver	Gall bladder
Spleen	Stomach
Lung	Large intestine
Kidneys	Bladder

The yin organs are regarded as those which store body materials – blood, fluids, *chi* – while the yang organs control functions. The yin organs are classified by the Chinese as being the heart, lungs, spleen, liver and kidneys, while the yang organs are the gall bladder, stomach, small intestine, large intestine, bladder and – a completely Chinese conception – the triple warmer which is not any specific organ but a controlling function which modifies the actions of a number of the other organs. The yin organs are yin both because they are regarded as storage organs and also because they are thought of as being deeper inside the body than the yang organs.

The heart is considered the ruler of the blood, but also the storage place of the spirit, a concept which exists also in the West, although not as a medical function. By tradition, the heart is considered to be closely connected with the tongue and therefore the Chinese doctor will diagnose from the state of the tongue how well the heart is fulfilling its functions. The heart is linked with the emotions of joy and excitement. A person who lives a joyless life is very likely to develop a damaged heart – in the West, we recognize this in our metaphor 'heartbroken'. Western doctors know the often joyless temperament which marks the sufferer from angina, palpitations and other symptoms of a malfunctioning heart and the Chinese doctor would say that it is not the illness which brings about the emotions necessarily, but it could well be the other way around. Conversely, too much joy can bring great shocks to the heart which are damaging or even fatal. We find an example of this in the person who finally achieves what he has always wanted, and then dies very soon afterwards. The joy overpowered the heart.

The lungs are recognized as the controllers of the air entering and leaving the body, but also as the controllers of *chi*. They are also considered to be closely linked with the large intestine which passes water out of the body, via the kidneys and bladder, and which also supplies the energy to work the bowels. Lungs have a connection with hair and skin, and shining healthy hair shows that the lungs are in good condition. Emotionally the lungs are associated with grief – sadness and grieving damage them if prolonged.

The spleen, according to the Chinese, is a somewhat different organ from the Western spleen. It is regarded as extracting nutrition from food and drink, out of which it creates blood and energy. It controls and regulates the composition of the blood, setting its levels of minerals and chemicals, rather like a treatment plant. It is the spleen which is considered to be the real source of an unborn baby's nutrition, and it also has a linked relationship with the stomach. If the two work in harmony – being yin and yang – digestion is excellent but, if there is disharmony, the nutritive elements from food will not be properly absorbed. Compulsive eaters who cannot control their appetite often seek acupuncture treatment since the acupuncturist can disrupt the relationship between spleen and stomach by inserting a needle into a point on the outer ear, so that less nutrients will be absorbed, and to change the pathological relationship between the two which has developed. The same can be true for anorexia nervosa, the compulsive non-eating which mainly affects teenage girls. Psychological treatment largely fails because this is not essentially a nervous affliction even though its origins may be. It is a physical abnormality in the relationship between spleen and stomach. The nervousness and withdrawn appearance of such girls is an emotional by-product of this, since the emotion associated with the malfunction of spleen and stomach is anxiety. Anorexics need treatment to right an imbalance of the body. The poor muscle tone of anorexics is also due to this, since the spleen controls muscle development by supplying the necessary nutrition.

The liver is classically regarded as the general of the body – it organizes the troops of blood and energy and sends them where they need to go. It enables everything to work smoothly and, when it is afflicted, nothing does. It is very sensitive and, when disrupted, the whole body feels it. It controls bile secretion and it also regulates the emotions. It is especially linked to anger which can badly damage the liver. On the other hand, a malfunctioning liver can give rise to anger and a person who habitually flies into sudden rages is almost certain to be diagnosed by the Chinese doctor as having a liver condition. The Chinese medical theory links the liver with the eyes and the tendons, tendons being understood as also including ligaments and some muscles. A person having eye trouble – irritation, red eyes, itching eyes – will be suspected of having a liver problem. In fact many contact-lens wearers find that their lenses are intensely irritating to wear at certain times, with no apparent cause. Even having their eyes checked reveals nothing, but the irritation continues. This is a sign that they should be thinking more about the condition of their liver. Women who wear contact lenses are often warned by their doctors that they may have problems wearing the lenses if they take the contraceptive pill.

Western doctors cannot definitively explain the reason why, except to say it is merely a known complication of the pill. However, in terms of Chinese medicine it is totally explicable. The contraceptive pill is known to cause the formation of gall stones, which means basically that they affect the function of the gall bladder. The gall bladder is the yang counterpart of the yin liver. The pill disrupts the function of the gall bladder, which disrupts the function of the liver, which in turn leads to eye problems.

The kidneys are regarded as the rulers of birth, development and growth. Although Western doctors note that the Chinese apparently did not know of the adrenal glands – which are attached to the kidneys – in fact it is largely merely a matter of vocabulary. The Chinese attributed to the kidneys the functions of controlling growth and say that the life *chi* is stored there. They are also, as in the West, regarded as controlling the water in the body, by processing it and passing it round the body and ultimately out of the body. Kidneys are linked with bone and by this reasoning Chinese doctors explain deafness in old people as being largely due to kidney malfunction. When the kidneys are malfunctioning, there is a certain amount of atrophy and shrinkage in the bones. This particularly affects bones like the sensitive tiny bones of the ear. Therefore some kinds of deafness are due to shrinkage of those bones so that they no longer touch and pass vibrations which can be recognized by the brain. The treatment for this is to build up kidney *chi* once more. Chinese doctors can successfully treat certain kinds of deafness with acupuncture because of this. Emotionally the kidneys are linked with fear, and it is likely that a child subject to continual fear will develop kidney disease. Kidneys are also linked with the head hair and it is due to weakness of the kidneys that people tend to lose their hair as they grow older.

The yang organs deal mainly with the reception, absorption and dispersal of food and each one is linked with a yin organ. The Chinese call this an interior-exterior relationship. The gall bladder stores and secretes bile and, as it is closely linked with the liver, any disturbance of either disrupts the smooth working of the other. The gall bladder, like the liver, is linked with anger, but especially the kind of anger which results in rash decisions. Weakness in the gall bladder may underlie indecisiveness and timidity.

The stomach receives and processes food and distributes it to the spleen where it is processed into use as blood and *chi* and is sent to the small intestine for further processing.

The small intestine continues digesting that which has been sent by the stomach and sends it further on to the large intestine where food is turned into faeces and discharged from the body.

The bladder receives and excretes urine. On the whole, the yang organ functions are perceived in much the same way as they are in the West. It is the yin organs which are significantly different. They are linked with their function and with the essential working of the body organs, whereas the yang organs are largely just processing mechanisms.

Another interesting aspect of the interchange of yin and yang comes in regard to the ageing of human beings. A male begins life as somewhat yin but mainly yang. His yangness develops to fullness with sexual maturity, when his voice loses its pre-adolescent lightness and physical sexuality begins to show. He maintains his yangness until old age when gradually he once more begins to become yin. In the female, the process is the other way round. As the woman ages, she begins to show developing yang – her voice becomes lower, she loses her specially feminine physical attributes and may even grow hair on her face. Finally, between a very old man and a very old woman there is often little to differentiate their sex in an obvious way. This is the expression in human life of the ever-changing cycle of yin and yang.

Table 2 *Yin and Yang – Physics*

yin	*yang*
matter	energy
night	day
earth	sky
slow	fast
weak	strong
down	up
inward	outward
stillness	motion
internal	external
cold	heat
winter	summer
water	fire
dark	bright
moon	sun
negative	positive

Table 3 *Yin and Yang – Physiology and Pathology*

Physiology

Sex	*Body parts*	*Tissues and organs*	*Condition/function*
Yin			
female	internal abdomen	blood, tendons, bone, heart, liver, spleen, lungs, kidneys	sedation, chronic, hypo-functional, degenerative
Yang			
male	external back	energy, skin, hair, small intestine, stomach, gall bladder, large intestine, bladder	stimulation, acute, hyper-function, generative

Pathology

Disease	*Pulse*
Yin	
cold, internal, chronic, deficient, degenerative, hypo-functional	deep, slow, weak, deficient
Yang	
hot, external, acute, excess, generative, hyper-functional	superficial, fast, strong, excess

The Five Elements

The Five Elements theory is basic to Chinese medicine but is little understood by Westerners, even those who actually practise Chinese medicine or acupuncture. This is largely due to the problem of translation, or rather to the fact that it is impossible in a direct translation to capture all the nuances contained in a single Chinese character. The Five Elements referred to are Wood, Fire, Earth, Metal and Water, but they are not so much the material substances that we would commonly associate with those five names as a reference to five kinds of process which explain the interaction of the physical world. It is really a description of how the material world changes.

In classical Chinese, the relationships of the Five Elements are usually demonstrated in the following way:

Fire burns Wood, which becomes ashes and these eventually become part of the Earth, in which Metal is found. When Metal is melted, it becomes to all appearances Water (i.e. liquid) and Water nourishes everything which grows, including the trees which in turn give us Wood, and so on. It is rather like that finger game which children play – paper wraps stone, stone breaks scissors, scissors cut paper and so on – which also comes from China.

In terms of disease, the Five Elements structure is used to characterize various diseases and the ways in

The Five Elements Chain of Reactions

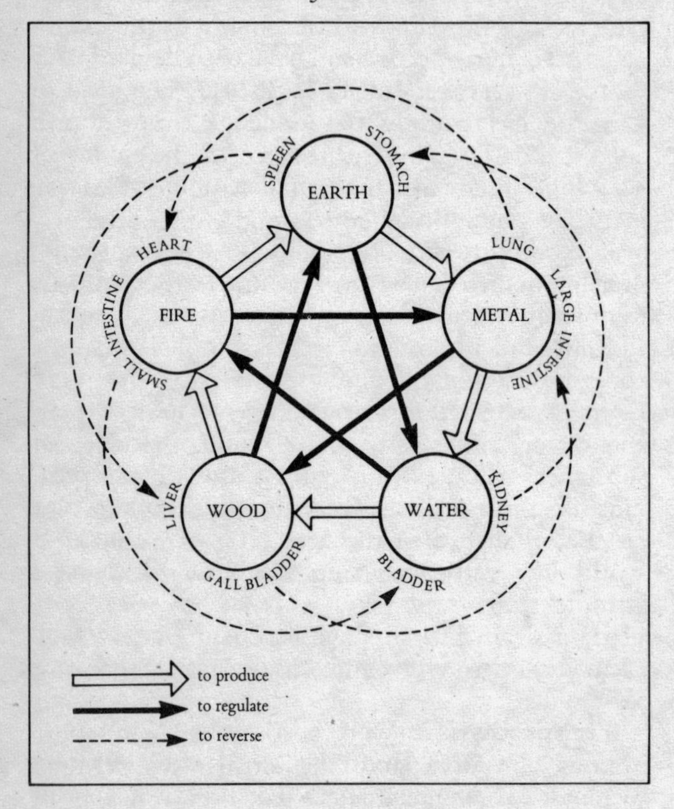

which they are cured or in which they attack human beings. It can be regarded largely as a metaphor, a form of explanation which fits diseases into the physical world. It does not really matter that the Westerner understands it, except just to realize that it is upon the observed harmonies and disharmonies of the Five Elements that Chinese doctors have based the way they explain much of their treatment. However, it must be said that many of the explanations are retrospective and have been devised later to explain the phenomena of disease. The ideal of harmony has to apply to knowledge as much as to any other part of Chinese life since it is the picture of the whole from which all smaller units of knowledge must be drawn.

According to the great Chinese scholar, Joseph Needham, it would be more accurate to describe the Five Elements as the Five Processes and it might help the reader to remember this. We shall continue to use the term Five Elements because it is the one in constant use. The processes referred to each have their own characteristic behaviour. Wood, for example, is the active growing process. Fire represents functions at their maximum height of activity, just before their decline. Metal represents functions in decline. Water refers to functions which have been at their most passive, ready to move into activity again. Earth seems to represent, not so much a specific function as the relationship between functions.

Each process is linked with a season – Wood with spring, Fire with summer, Metal with autumn, Water with winter. Again Earth represents the transition between each season.

The recurring cycle of five is a frequent one in Chinese culture. There are five tastes – sour, bitter, sweet, metallic and salty. There are five emotions – anger, joy, anxiety, grief and fear. There are five colours – blue (or green, since both are often perceived as the same colour by the Chinese), red, yellow, white and black. There are five directions –

Table 4 *The Five Elements As They Affect Nature*

Five Elements	*Wood*	*Fire*	*Earth*	*Metal*	*Water*
Natural develop-ment	birth	growth	transformation	collection	storage
Colour	green	red	yellow	white	black
Taste	sour	bitter	sweet	metallic	salty
Season	spring	summer	late summer	autumn	winter
Climate	windy	hot	humid	dry	cold

Table 5 *The Five Elements As They Affect Man*

	Wood	*Fire*	*Earth*	*Metal*	*Water*
Yin organs	liver	heart	spleen	lungs	kidneys
Yang organs	gall bladder	small intes-tine	stomach	large intes-tine	bladder
Body tissues	tendon	blood vessels	muscle	skin, hair	bone
Sensory organs	eyes	tongue	mouth	nose	ears
Emotions	anger	joy, excitement	anxiety	grief	fear

north, south, east, west and, with obvious logic, centre. There are five kinds of climate – windy, hot, dry, humid and cold. Quite why five was so important we no longer can be sure, but numerology was extremely important in early Chinese culture, certainly among the many mystical cults of early times, and it is obviously something to do with that. Groups of five were connected with the classification of things on the earth or material things, while other groups – mainly six, four and three – were used to classify the things of heaven or the spirit.

It must be said that to apply the Five Elements theory to every phase of disease requires some ingenuity. Historically the Five Elements theory and the yin and yang theory were not connected with each other. They were two independent schools of thought as far back as the third and fourth centuries BC and it was not until the Sung dynasty (AD 960–1279) that we find the two being fully interconnected. The best reason for using the Five Elements theory is that it is a good way to organize and explain observable clinical data, and that is why most practitioners use it.

Chi

Chi is a word often used by people as if it were some mysterious, almost mystical force known only to the Chinese and a few other select members of a brotherhood of secret understanding. This is a pity since the character which represents *chi* basically means energy. Having said that, it is only fair to acknowledge the complications of understanding *chi*. One Western authority on Chinese medicine, Doctor Manfred Porket, says he can find nine major shades of meaning in *chi*, proceeds to describe thirty-two more, and indicates that the list could well have continued. *Chi* is very commonly used in Chinese medicine to mean life, air, energy, breath and disease, and to describe a numb tingling in the body. For our general purposes, it is sufficient to understand *chi* as energy and to know that its main functions are to act as a harmonizer in the body and to transform matter to energy. For example, when nutrients are processed into energy, it is *chi* which is the fuel for the process of change.

The Chinese recognize that there are many kinds of energy and, being extremely precise observers, have named and catalogued them all. For example, they regard each major organ of the body as having its own particular kind of *chi* – there is heart energy, lung energy and so on. It is perhaps this which Western medicine describes very vaguely as 'the will to live', a known part of recovery and yet a very

Table 6 *Blood and Chi. Common Symptoms of Imbalance*

Chi	*Blood*
Deficiency:	
Shortness of breath, cold sweats, quiet, low voice, cold extremities, poor appetite, tense muscles, soft stools or diarrhoea, ringing in the ears, dizziness, palpitations, fatigue, tremors, numbness in hands and feet, sleeps a lot	Pale face and lips, restless and irritable, suffers from insomnia, fatigue, dryness in mouth and nostrils, night sweating, cramp and twisted muscles, poor vision, constipation
Tongue – pale, dilated, wet, thin white coating	*Tongue* – dark with bluish tinge, dry, no coating
Pulse – slow, weak, sluggish	*Pulse* – fast, weak, tight
Excess:	
Tight chest, dyspnoea, distension of stomach, chest pains, belching, hiccoughs, constipation, fever, pains in the ribs, headaches, blurred vision, irritable, asthmatic	Headaches, dizziness, pains in the body, muscle spasms, fever, restless, hysteria, red lips, red eyes, blood in urine or stool, strokes
Tongue – solid, dry, yellow coating	*Tongue* – dark red, dry, no coating
Pulse – superficial, fast, strong	*Pulse* – superficial, fast, strong

woolly term. The Chinese would regard someone with, for example, a serious heart condition and no will to live as simply having used up their heart *chi* and therefore being beyond recovery. On the whole, the *chi* of most major organs is renewable, except for kidney *chi* as we have already explained, but if it falls below a certain level then it can no longer be increased. The result of major *chi* deficiency is death.

The major kinds of *chi* influencing health are classified as Original *chi*, Organic *chi*, Meridian *chi*, *ying chi*, *wai chi* and *tsong chi*.

Original chi

This is the nutritional energy of the kidneys and it is derived from food, drink and oxygen. It is circulating energy which travels throughout the body and acts as the triggering energy for the body mechanisms. It is also this which acts as the disease resistance factor and controls immunity. It regulates the physiological functions.

Organic chi

This is the original *chi* within the major body organs, which harmonizes the functions of the organs.

Meridian chi

This is the energy which circulates in the meridians and which carries the whole-body communication which is the purpose of the meridian system. After an acupuncture needle has been inserted into one of the meridians, the sensation which the patient feels is called *dai chi*, which means 'getting the energy'.

Ying chi

This is nutritive *chi* and it is part of the blood and derived from food and drink. It supplies nutrition to all parts of the body by way of the meridians and also acts as an internal defence system against disease.

Wai chi

This is also known as the guardian *chi* and it circulates outside the meridians on the outer surface of the body, forming an external barrier against disease. It has a thermal regulating effect, warming or cooling the body according to the weather or the environment. It regulates the functions of muscles, skin and hair.

Tsong chi

This is combined *chi* which gathers at the chest and goes out of the body via the throat. It regulates the cardiac and respiratory system, affecting also the voice and the level of physical stamina.

Acupuncture and the Meridian System

The meridian system, upon which acupuncture is presumed to work, is known as the *Ching luo* in Chinese. This can be translated as 'a silken network of pathways' which effectively describes the way in which the traditional healer thinks of the meridians. In Western medicine, whole-body communication is only believed to take place via the neuro system, but the Chinese consider that there is a second whole-body communication system which is made up of the vascular and lymphatic systems working together as one electrical energy network.

This network, which can be measured on electronic apparatus, has three basic functions. Firstly, it is one way in which man is connected with the electro-magnetic energy field in which he lives and which surrounds him. This energy field has been extensively demonstrated in recent decades through phenomena like the Kirlian photographic experiments which show how human beings, and indeed all animate objects, emit energy. Secondly, the meridian system is a way of controlling this energy field, of regulating the supply and flow of electrical energy to and from all the body organs and, thirdly, it is itself a communication network through which information is passed to and from the body cells.

The numerous points on the meridian system

have been plotted from areas of sensitivity which originally were noted as being connected with certain disorders. In the year 1000 BC some 132 of these points had been noted, but now the acupuncturist works from a network of over 600 points altogether, of which about 365 are of major significance. Research in China since 1958 has resulted in another 200 or more points being added to the network, and doubtless others will follow as more are discovered.

However, from the practising acupuncturist's point of view, there are twelve vitally important meridians, each linked to a major organ of the body, plus eight subsidiary meridians which are also of importance. Each meridian runs from top to toe and along the arms and, when an acupuncture needle is inserted at a pressure point, it creates an energy surge which clears any blockage which has formed and brings energy flooding through the network. The points of importance along the meridians are well charted and every acupuncturist has the task of learning exactly where they can all be found before he can do his work.

It is assumed that acupuncture originated in Neanderthal times as people began to observe that pressure massage helped to reduce localized pain. Gradually, they also noticed that heat could be used for healing and sedative purposes, and it is from these two observations that the present complex system has evolved. Iron needles for acupuncture purposes were used fairly early on in Chinese history, taking over from flint, bone and bamboo implements. The actual name acupuncture derives from the Latin – *acus punctura* which literally means

Acupuncture Meridians

The acupuncture meridians are networks of points running throughout the body, each relating to a specific organ. By pressing on these points, an energy surge is created which clears blockages in the energy network and stimulates the organ into a healthy balance of function once more. The meridians have been charted from early times and these examples are drawn from a Ming dynasty medical text. However, even today the meridian network is still being researched and extended.

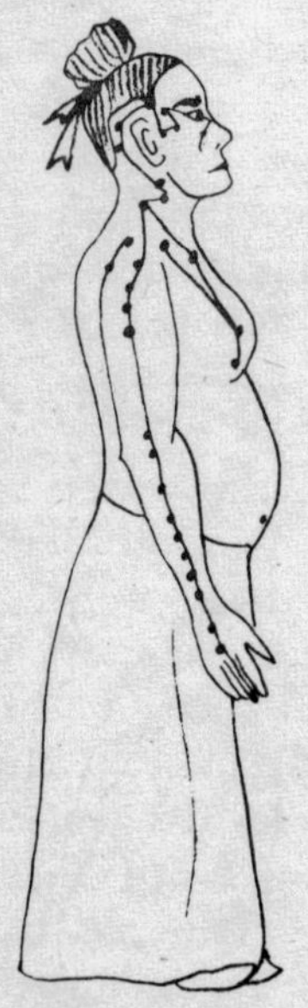

Triple warmer

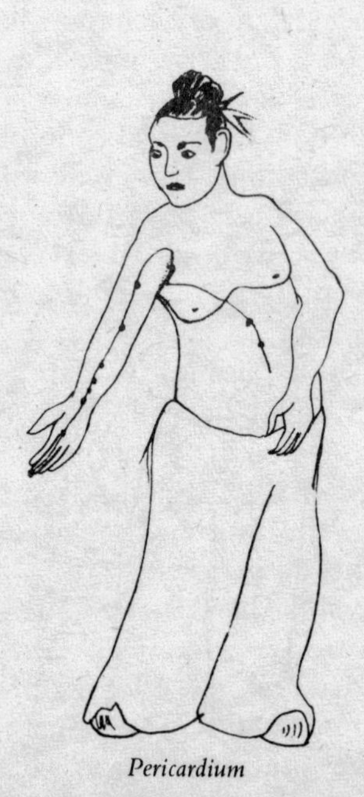

Pericardium

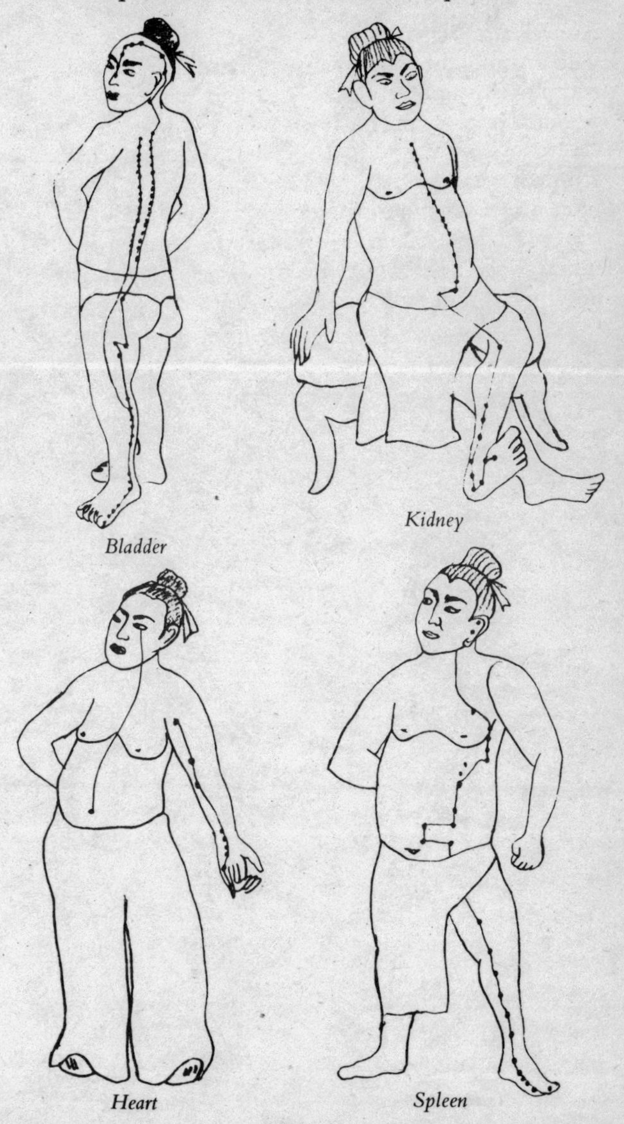

Bladder

Kidney

Heart

Spleen

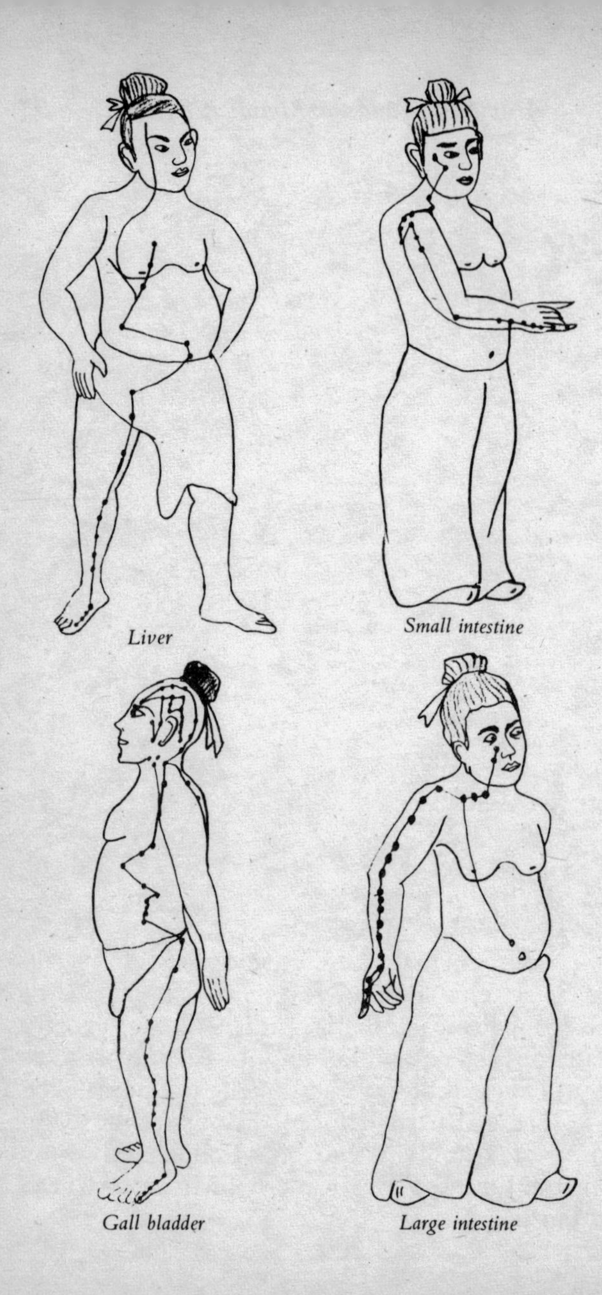
Liver
Small intestine
Gall bladder
Large intestine

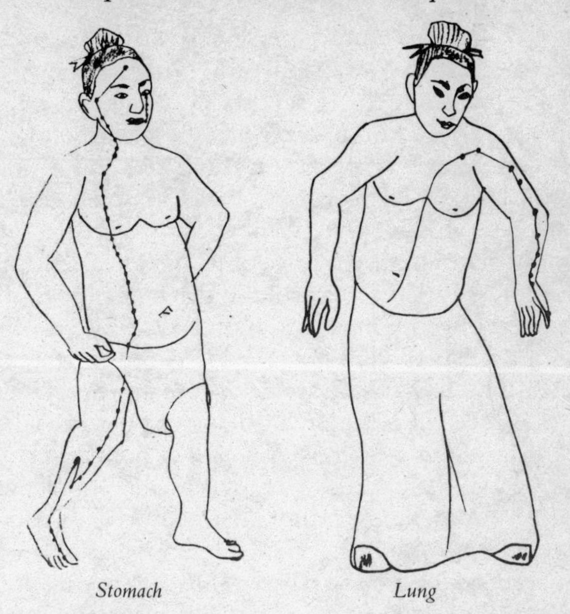

Stomach *Lung*

'needle puncture'. These days the needles are extremely fine and slender, much more so than even the smallest sewing needle, and when they are inserted at a pressure point they are felt as a slight pain which soon passes or even as a tingling numbness.

Most acupuncturists also use moxibustion to help treatment. This means lighting a cigar-fat roll of herbal medicine, looking rather like a grossly inflated joss stick, and holding it over the pressure point. This is thought to stimulate the point even more. The herb used in this medicine stick is usually *Artemesia vulgaris*, and the term moxibustion comes from the Japanese *Moe Kusa*, which means 'herb that burns'.

Critics of acupuncture say that there is no evidence that it works, but frankly this is nonsense. There are numerous reports of its use in experiments carried out in a completely scientific manner in China, in Europe and in the USA, and these are available for anyone who cares to follow up the subject. Most people, if they know anything at all about acupuncture, know of its use as a pain-killer. Either they have read about the many operations carried out in China, often under the eyes of Western observers who have been invited to watch, or they may have come across its use in pain clinics in the West. The Chinese use acupuncture anaesthesia because they feel it is much less damaging than using gases and leads to a much smaller incidence of surgical shock. Even the most complex open-heart operations can be carried out under acupuncture anaesthesia, with the patient fully conscious. In the West, pain clinics have begun to use acupuncture for the control of pain, although unfortunately such use is all too often carried out by doctors with no training at all in the use of acupuncture and therefore little knowledge of what they are really doing. Even so, they still get results.

However, because acupuncture has not been explored very fully in the West, its other great benefits in treatment are either ignored or simply not known about. Often Western doctors are reluctant to try it because they do not understand why it works. Its use as a pain-killer is explained as either breaking the transmission of pain messages or perhaps releasing pain-muffling endomorphines in the brain. This is a pity since acupuncture can be successful in treating a whole range of other conditions, many of them not easily cured in Western medicine. Among these can be migraine, hay fever, asthma, arthritis, some forms of deafness, eczema, paralysis, excessive sweating, trigeminal neuralgia (tic douloureux) and many back conditions which otherwise do not respond to treatment. It works, say Chinese practitioners, not because acupuncture has some secret power, but rather because many Western medical conditions are not examined as a complete syndrome of symptoms integrated in a particular individual's body, but as isolated occurrences.

Since this is not a book of acupuncture, we shall not go into great depth here but would point out that, just as food affects the whole body, so also does it affect the various meridians. A weakness in a particular meridian can often be treated by taking appropriate foods, so we append here a table of the syndrome of symptoms typical of meridian problems.

Table 7 *Meridian Imbalance. A Table of Symptoms*

Meridian	*Excess syndrome (yang)*	*Deficiency syndrome (yin)*
Lung	shoulder pains, headaches, palpitations, heartburn, cough	heavy breathing, short of breath, dry throat, dry skin, thirst, cold extremities
Large intestine	frozen shoulder, toothache, headache, haemorrhoids	irregular bowels, diarrhoea, frozen shoulder, dry throat, irritability

Table 7 (*cont.*)

Meridian	*Excess syndrome (yang)*	*Deficiency syndrome (yin)*
Stomach	dry lips, hiccoughing, excessive appetite, arthritis pains, mastitis	yawning, poor appetite, abdominal pain, heaviness in extremities, swollen face, depression
Spleen	lower abdomen swollen, vomiting, arthritis in the legs, cold feet, indigestion	diarrhoea, nausea, belching, swollen painful abdomen, easily tired
Heart	swallowing air into stomach, constipation, weakness of extremities, dry throat, heart disease	heart pains, palpitations, yellow eyeballs, uneasiness, diarrhoea
Small intestine	abdominal distention, stomach pain, tight chest, headaches	headaches, ringing in the ears, poor hearing, feeling cold
Bladder	headaches, stiff neck, back pains, numbness in feet, pains in the feet, eyestrain	stiff neck, back pains, numbness in feet, pains in feet, upper back pains, depression
Kidneys	diseases of the sexual organs, dry throat, pain in the abdomen, hot feet	lack of sexual drive, restless, easily tired, poor memory, general weakness, dizziness, poor appetite, poor hearing, aches and pains in the joints
Pericardium	angina, pain in left shoulder, bloodshot eyes	palpitations, tight chest, cold sweaty hands

Table 7 *(cont.)*

Meridian	*Excess syndrome (yang)*	*Deficiency syndrome (yin)*
Triple warmer	lower part of the abdomen swollen and hard, abnormal urination, ringing in the ears, poor hearing	indigestion, breathing difficulties, low fever, fatigue
Gall bladder	heavy head, headaches, no appetite, quick temper	dizziness, weak eyes, poor vision, heaviness in extremities, unsteady on the feet
Liver	bloodshot eyes, eye infections, pain in the penis, abnormal menstruation, chest pains, anger, over-excitable, glaucoma, cataracts, pain in the ribs	hard distended stomach, giddiness on standing up, lack of sexual drive, prolapse of anus

Human Types

The Chinese have a number of different ways of classifying human beings, depending upon the field of knowledge being applied. For example, people can be arranged in types according to their facial features, the art of reading the face being considered far more important in traditional Chinese society than that of reading the palm. People can be classified according to their strata in society or according to the relationship in which they stand to another person – Confucianism is largely built around the correctness of the great relationships which make a society. Teacher and student, parent and child, emperor and subject, and so on. Doctors too have their own system of classifying people and they do it firstly by body type, and then by yin and yang.

The four main body types, according to Chinese medical theory, are thoracic, abdominal, cardiac and neuro, and each of these can be either yin or yang, although both abdominal and cardiac types have a strong natural tendency towards being yang. Each body type is designated after its most important physical feature, and virtually everyone fits fairly obviously into one of them. It will not be very hard to establish which one you are after considering the guidelines below.

Thoracic Type

In appearance, thoracic types are thin and have, as their name suggests, a long thorax. This gives them a very good chest with large healthy lungs unconstricted by any other parts of the body. A thoracic person is literally a windbag, with powerful lungs – so you are likely to find this person talking or singing a lot and not very quietly either. This is also a good candidate for marathon running.

However, because the long thorax tends to push down on the digestive organs, the thoracic type suffers throughout his life from digestive problems. He is very liable to have stomach ulcers and gastrointestinal disorders, and it is these which will lead eventually to his death if he does not make an effort to come to terms with his strengths and weaknesses and act accordingly. The thoracic person must always pay special attention to diet, and should always eat food which is easy to digest, avoiding anything which will distress an already disadvantaged digestive system. That said, this is otherwise a healthy type who can expect a good long life.

Thoracic types can be yin or yang.

Abdominal Type

Abdominal types are easy to spot – big generous stomachs, stout or positively chubby in build, with good muscles. Their over-developed stomachs take up the space needed for their thorax, and therefore they have small and somewhat inadequate lungs. This means a natural tendency towards weakness in the respiratory system and chest diseases in general, but not usually including tuberculosis. Because the stomach is using up lung space, the abdominal type easily gets short of breath, especially when he over-eats, which he often does.

This situation can become further complicated by poor pulmonary circulation, which in turn leads to cardiac problems, especially as these types tend towards over-eating and over-weight.

Obviously, abdominal types should curb their natural greed and avoid both over-eating and their craving for rich foods. In fact, following a vegetarian diet is the healthiest way for the abdominal type to eat. He should also endeavour to increase the capacity of his lungs by doing breathing exercises. If there are colds and influenza around, he must do his utmost to avoid them as he is prone to serious respiratory complications and can easily get pneumonia.

Hypertension and cholesterol are his biggest enemies. Although it is possible to find a yin abdominal type, if you look very hard, most of these plump high-living abdominals are yang.

Cardiac Type

These are also rather ominously known as stroke types. They are fat, with short necks, large bellies and short arms and legs. When they laugh, their already red faces get redder; especially their ears. Because the stomach and intestines have plenty of room, cardiac types have excellent digestion. Their digestive systems are very efficient and thoroughly absorb all the nutrients from the large quantities of food they eat. This is why they gain weight so easily. Their lungs are usually in good shape, but their heart tends to be constricted for space and their major blood vessels are thin and not very powerful.

Cardiac people tend to be clumsy and therefore tend to dislike any kind of sport or exercise, other than that gained by lifting food to the mouth. However, if they do not control their eating and also take mild exercise, they are in grave danger of having strokes. They suffer greatly from hypertension and many heart problems, and would be greatly helped by the mild gentle exercise that walking could give them. Tai Chi Ch'uan, the Taoist practice of formalized exercises, would also be very beneficial. They should never take part in violent exercise like tennis or jogging.

These excitable and impulsive people are virtually always yang.

Neuro Type

This is also known as the nervous type, though they need not be nervous at all. These people are usually thin, with large heads and long necks. Their fingers and toes are also long and thin – they have the look that is often described as artistic, which indeed many of them are. They tend to be pale-faced and can be neurotic and self-obsessed. Their hearts and lungs are normal, but their stomachs are small and they often eat little. Many neuro types suffer from insomnia due to over-active minds.

These can be either yin or yang. Yin neuro people seem cool and unemotional on the surface because their sensitive feelings are concealed. They are introverts and can suffer suicidal depressions. Yang neuro types, on the other hand, can be restless, irritable, critical and with a certain current of hysteria running beneath all this. They also suffer from bouts of insomnia and can swing violently from tears to laughter. This unpredictability can make them dangerous.

Since neuro people are very sensitive, it is very important that they pay special attention to their eating. More than the other types, they have the capacity to control and change what they are through the careful application of food therapy and their systems are responsive. Many of the people who die from drug addiction are neuro types who sought to control their lives through changing their awareness of the pain they feel. However, they must learn instead to control their sensitivities through food since their systems respond well to this.

Yang neuro types must avoid any further stimulants. They need plenty of vitamin C, which has a calming effect, fruit, vegetables, but no spicy food and no high mineral tablets such as iron or potassium, since these only serve to excite the system further. They must avoid chocolate, coffee, wines and spirits and only drink cooling and calming drinks, like jasmine tea.

Yin neuro types, on the other hand, need stimulation. Their kidneys are often deficient in strength, which is the underlying factor in depression, and they need to eat and drink food good for the kidneys. Red wine and brandy are both good for them, as are ginseng, spicy foods, some meat but little vitamin C. Vitamin C makes the body very cold and depresses the natural functions of the organs.

Since the nervous system is intimately related to kidney function, neuro types often suffer from kidney troubles and can finally die of kidney diseases.

The majority of those who commit suicide or

murder fit into the neuro type category since the weakness of their kidneys – and therefore their nervous systems – makes them particularly prone to acts of excess due to emotional causes. This is why it is especially important for neuro types to take responsibility for their own well-being, knowing their weaknesses as they do.

You may well read through all of these types and find that you do not seem to fit into any category. In that case, you are obviously a combined type and must find the two categories which, put together, best describe you. If you have to do this, pay special attention to the descriptions of your emotional behaviour, as this will probably be most related to your health profile. It is not at all unusual to find that you are a combined type and it has advantages – you have twice the number of strengths to call upon, although you also have to guard your health on two counts as well. For more thorough guidance on diet, read the food chapter.

Once you have sorted out which of these types basically describes you, the next thing you have to do is to decide whether you are a yin or a yang of your type. Again, most people tend to be fairly definitely either yin or yang, but this can vary according to their state of health or other factors which can bring about changes. The table below summarizes the basic characteristics of yin and yang people. Not all will apply to you and, of those that do apply, very few will apply all the time. Look for the description which tends to fit you in a general sense and that is likely to be your type. Remember that illness and other factors can cause change, and check the table again if you feel that you are changing. It will help you to spot the onset of disharmony before it progresses to actual illness and, by referring to the later chapters on food and drink, you will be able to help yourself.

Table 8 *Are You Yin or Yang?*

Characteristic	*Yin*	*Yang*
Typical behaviour	introverted, easily tired, sleeps curled up, often closes eyes, prefers the shade, suffers from depression, often looks sad or worried, over-controlled	excitable, restless, irritable, active, eyes wide open and alert, stretches frequently
Physique	slightly built, weak, movements lack energy	large build, strong, energetic
Complexion	pale, sallow but occasionally with red spots on the cheeks	red-faced, blushes easily, eyes often inflamed
Body temperature	low, often has cold hands and feet, tendency to run a low temperature in the afternoons	warm skin, hands and feet, easily develops fevers
Sensitivities	enjoys massage, often has numbness or dull pains in the body, itchiness	gets severe stabbing pains, hot flushes, dislikes massage, burning sensations in the body
Muscle tone	weak flabby muscles, little flesh	muscular, tense muscles, very active

Table 8 *(cont.)*

Characteristic	*Yin*	*Yang*
Respiration	weak, shallow, often short of breath	heavy breathing, tight chest
Eating pattern	poor appetite, suffers indigestion, likes warm food and drink	good appetite, excellent digestion, likes cold food and drink
Bowels	soft stools, tendency to diarrhoea, undigested food passed in stools	constipation, hard stools, burning sensation in the anus
Urination	frequent, can lose control of urination, clear in colour	infrequent, difficulty in passing urine, yellow in colour
Sweating	cold, light	hot or no sweating at all
Menstruation	blood light in colour, often late, small flow, pain after period is over	dark heavy flow, often clotted, usually early or less than 28-day cycle, pain before flow starts
Palpation of abdomen	soft, feels no discomfort	hard, tense, painful
Tongue	pale, dilated, covered with thin white coating, insensitive	red, dry, solid-looking, thick coating, very sensitive
Pulse	weak, slow	strong, fast

Part Three

Today's Special Medical Problems

A whole range of common conditions is dealt with elsewhere in this book, but there are a few which are considered particularly special to our own times and social climate which we examine here. Although this section contains some specific suggestions for dietary additions or changes, the general guidelines set up in detail elsewhere will still, of course, apply. Therefore, after reading this section, the reader will find further help in the dietary patterns outlined in other chapters. It should be borne in mind that we cannot guarantee the results which we indicate are possible here, but we hope you try to tackle these problems according to the diagnosis and explanation given in Chinese medicine. It may well be of interest that in some instances the same explanation is now being put forward by Western medical practitioners – good examples are the problem of hyperactive children and why there are so many these days, and the issue of picking your child's sex through your own and your partner's dietary choice.

Impotence

It is not unusual that impotence is often a natural part of increasing old age, when many men are not particularly troubled by it, having already accepted or indeed accelerated for themselves the idea that age means impotence. According to the Chinese, it is not age itself that causes impotence but the degenerative changes of the kidneys, remembering that in Chinese medicine kidney means not just the excretory organs we think of in the West, but the whole growth functions attached to them – adrenal, hormonal and control of nervous energy, all of which are considered to derive from the state of the kidneys.

However, an alarming feature of life today is the number of young men affected by impotence. Men who otherwise seem to be fit, healthy and ordinarily happy are quietly admitting to impotence and, if they are not admitting it, today's women are beginning to notice how many men fail to achieve or maintain erections. This problem seems to peak in men aged from twenty-five to thirty-five, and Chinese traditional doctors are finding this among their patients just as much as Western doctors are.

There are a number of causes of impotence according to the Chinese:

Too much sexual activity is considered to lead to impotence because it depletes kidney energy which supplies the fuel for sexual activity. This is undoubtedly one of the major causes of impotence in young previously highly active men. Impotence is one way in which the body acts to protect its resources and, while it has been very fashionable to regard impotence in the West as almost entirely psychological, this view is not fully supported by Chinese medical opinion.

Another cause can indeed be mental stress, however. An over-active brain puts the body under stress and this in turn depletes the nervous system.

The energy for the nervous system comes from the kidneys, as does sexual energy, and therefore again the body acts to conserve that rapidly disappearing energy. In terms of survival, although human beings rate sexual activity very highly, the body itself recognizes that it is not in the front line of physical survival, and it is one of the functions which the body will jettison when more urgent physical priorities arise.

Psychological factors are included in the possible causes of impotence, with fear being the main one. Fear is the emotion associated with the kidneys, therefore any situation involving feelings of fear may affect potency. This does not necessarily indicate fear of sexual situations, although that may well be a factor, but could equally be a reflection of fear in some other life situation, the effects of which are carrying over into sexual activity. These fears could be job fears, anxiety about family situations, moving to another town and any of the variety of scenarios in which anxiety underlies what is happening.

The most likely cause of all, in the opinion of Chinese doctors, is bad eating. Foods which sedate the actions of the body organs too much will also affect functions and reduce their activity.

A man who is afflicted with impotence should start paying close attention to what he eats. He should avoid an excess of calming or cooling foods and, for a more comprehensive list of these, he should turn to the food chapter. To be particularly avoided are grapefruit and lemon juice – both extremely sedating to the body. Another item to exclude is beer, because it contains hops which are also very sedating and have the effect of suppressing the function of the adrenal glands. Other items to cut out of the diet for a while are cabbage, celery, broccoli and radish, while foods which will help to build up sexual energy are eggs, shrimps and all kinds of meats such as chicken, pigeon, beef and lamb. Mussels, oysters, peanuts and walnuts are all considered particularly tonifying for the kidneys.

Hyperactive children

The syndrome of the hyperactive child has become only too familiar to medical practitioners, psychologists and educationalists in the past few years, and efforts to treat hyperactivity have covered a whole range of approaches, some of them very disturbing in their implications, such as the use of barbiturates to control behaviour. Unfortunately this does not so much treat the condition as keep the child sedated. It is aimed at the symptoms, not at the underlying condition. However, the latest and rather encouraging news about hyperactivity is that it seems closely connected with diet, a discovery with which the Chinese traditional doctor would certainly agree.

Hyperactivity is fairly new on our medical horizon, and that is largely because of the extreme dietary changes undergone by children in the West in the last twenty years. In Chinese medical terms, hyperactive children are over-heated – that is, over-stimulated by too much of the wrong sort of food. A child in this state is restless, hot-tempered, lacks any attention span and seems tense and emotionally on edge. He finds it hard to keep still or to concentrate on anything, even playing, and he displays all the over-heated symptoms – irritability, mental excitement and physical unease.

The kinds of foods which over-stimulate the child's system are animal fats, yoghurt, pâté, cocoa, chocolate, fried potatoes, potato crisps, all kinds of fried, deep-fried, roasted, toasted and grilled food. All high-sugar soft drinks are included in this list. The stimulation which this overload brings into the child's system cannot be balanced out in a very young body and causes the metabolism to run even faster. Even if the diet is not changed, many hyperactive children eventually begin to come to balance as they approach puberty simply because their body systems have become stronger and their metabolism has slowed down. However, of those who do not come to a state of reasonable harmony, many may go on to become hyperactive adults, and it is this type which is most likely to be found among violent and criminal adults committing robberies and the pointless acts of random assault which can be one of the most alarming aspects of, for example, American life. The pop culture diet leads to this, and the same pattern is being repeated in Britain with the arrival of the American-style fast-food diet of hamburgers, French fries and carbonated soft drinks. Diet has much more to do with the radical change in urban violence and crime than with any sociological factors, in the opinion of Chinese medical experts.

Parents owe it to their children to pay much closer attention to what they eat. It is surprising how many caring parents who otherwise give great attention to every other aspect of their children's lives do not think it important to supervise the food their children eat. This is partly because in the West we have given comparatively little weight to matters of diet, unless we actually want to reduce our size, and also because of widespread ignorance about food. We are unaware of how profoundly our natural food pattern has changed in the last fifty years. We do not realize that what we are eating bears only an outward resemblance to the real thing – yoghurt full of chemical additives and with no live culture in it, vegetables with all the things we think we are eating them for actually processed out of them. Even when we hear that this is so, most people think it is only the crank who gets heated about the quality or naturalness of the food he eats. This is all part of our ignorance about what that food does to us when we eat it. Most people know more about how it feels to eat an aspirin than how their regular diet affects them. This is the unlucky fate of hyperactive children. All too often they are created by ignorant parents.

Most children are physically addicted to the foods which do most harm to them. Therefore, the parent will have to be determined to control that addiction, since the child himself cannot do so. Children – and indeed many adults – hate to change their diet, and this is even more true when they are built around imbalance. However, if your child is hyperactive and you want to save him and your family life from the destructiveness that goes with it, you must stick to his diet. If he were ill, you would do whatever was necessary to cure him. Hyperactivity is basically a food illness.

It will be necessary to supervise your child's diet

fairly strictly during the time of change-over and to resist all pleas for 'just one' of anything. Regard all such foods and drinks as causing an illness in your child and you will be able to hold out against any pleading and try to get your child to understand the same. You should be able to see some results within even a couple of months, but it could take longer. Be prepared for a six-month siege.

Conception

When a couple experience problems in conception and, after considerable medical investigation, no apparent cause is shown, the relevant factor may well be the temperature of the woman's womb. This is influenced by her diet, and therefore it can also be changed by altering her diet. The temperature is either too hot or too cold and either of these conditions can lead to lack of conception.

A woman whose womb is too hot for the sperm to survive must avoid all stimulating foods. This means no spicy food, few meats and none which have been roasted, grilled, barbecued or fried. For a full list, see the food chapter and avoid anything listed as stimulating. Instead, the woman should eat cooling foods, concentrating on vegetables and fruit. Items which are especially cooling include bananas, pears, watermelons, broccoli, turnips, grapefruit and, if it is possible to get them, gingko nuts. In fact, gingko nuts are considered to be so cooling for the womb that in ancient times courtesans and prostitutes ate them or took them in the form of tea in order to make sure that they did not become pregnant.

Conversely, a woman suffering from a womb which is too cold may already be following a diet which is too sedating and she must begin to eat stimulating foods instead. Again, there is a long list of these in the food chapter, but items which are especially good for heating up the womb again are lamb, beef, chicken, pig's liver, dates and red beans.

In order to decide whether or not this might be a factor in your case, check out the yin-yang table and see which is your predominant nature. If you are yang, although it is theoretically possible that you could have a cold womb, it is much more likely that over-heating is your problem, and vice-versa for a yin woman. Give the diet time to become established and to fit in with your own fertility cycle – say, a three-month period of time, at least.

Although there are many factors which decide whether a baby will be male or female, nevertheless ancient Chinese wisdom suggests that it is possible to decide the sex of your child in advance through certain food patterns. The fact that very many people in China today would dearly like to choose to have a boy as their one and only child, but get a girl instead, suggests that people now are not very much in touch with the old ways of thinking. Interestingly enough, this is yet another area in which the West and the East are coming into agreement, although by very different pathways. The Chinese say that the choice of sex depends upon whether the sperm are yin or yang, while in the West it is said that an acidic environment is preferred by females and alkaline by males. Acid is yin and alkaline is yang.

Both partners have to take part in the diet to

create the right ambience for the child of their choice. If the couple wish to have a boy, the husband should follow a very yang diet and the wife a very yin one. The yang diet should be full of protein, plenty of meat, fish and eggs and low in vegetables and fruit. At the same time, the woman should be concentrating on vegetables, fruit, milk, seaweed, beancurd, turnips, carrots, lettuce, vitamin C and calcium. She should avoid too many proteins. Both partners should follow the diet to comfort level – even in following a yin or yang diet, moderation is still the key.

Again a reasonable amount of time should be allowed for the diet to have affected the body before trying for conception. At least one month and preferably two should go by before the partners could reasonably hope for results from this guidance. By the way, we do not guarantee results – since there are other factors which can also change the individual to yin or yang, but we would be most interested to hear from those who feel that it has worked, especially if previous children were of a different sex.

Part Four

Food

Harmony may be illustrated by soup. You have the water and fire, vinegar, pickle, salt, and plums, with which to cook fish and meat. It is made to boil by the firewood, then the cook mixes the ingredients, harmoniously equalizing the several flavours, so as to supply whatever is deficient and carry off whatever is in excess. Then the master eats it, and his mind is made equable.

(Trans. Legge, 1872)

The above passage is said to come from a conversation which took place in 521 BC between the Marquis of Ch'i and the philosopher Tzu Yu. The two men were actually discussing something quite different – they were debating the meaning of harmony and dissent – but the fact that they chose the kitchen as their battleground and food as their weapon demonstrates how important the whole matter of correctly prepared food was, even then. It is really no different today. The Chinese cook does not merely drop ingredients into the wok without a thought. He works from a 3000-year history of a tradition which puts harmony up as the first item on any menu. It is probably hard to equate the average offerings of your nearest Chinese takeaway food shop with anything so grand as that. It is even more difficult to imagine that it also applies to the sweaty man in a grubby T-shirt who stands over a bubbling wok in a Hong Kong street, the delicious aroma of his work fighting against the curtain of carbon monoxide from the traffic. However, even the most humble practitioner of the art of Chinese cooking draws upon this long tradition, which has been absorbed since childhood in his mother's and grandmother's kitchens.

The harmony of the Chinese cuisine comes not only from the ingredients themselves, but also from a consideration of the eater and his requirements and even the season of the year. All of these things are ideally put together to make a meal which will 'make the mind equable', to quote the ancient philosopher. We use the word ideally because we recognize that unfortunately harmony may not always be the first intention of a restaurateur – he may just want to make a fast penny. But there is a thoroughly developed sophisticated system of harmonizing food which can be utilized by anyone who wishes to become familiar with it.

All food can be put into one of three categories, and these are usually translated by the terms 'heating', 'cooling' and 'neutral'. However, we feel these words are not satisfactory in that they are somewhat misleading and also limit the real meaning of the Chinese characters for the categories. Food which is heating in many cases does not raise the temperature of the body, although sometimes it will, while cooling food does not necessarily lower the temperature. Therefore, we prefer to use the words 'stimulating' and 'calming' instead, since we feel that describes their affect on functions far better. Stimulating food is that which stimulates your body system, and too much may push your body organs into over-production or excess. Calming food does the opposite – it has a sedative effect on the organs and influences them to function in a more yin way. Similarly, it is possible to overdo this and to depress the function of the organs, making them sluggish and deficient. Both excess and deficient states must be avoided if harmony is to rule – and that is what choosing food and drink wisely is all about. Neutral foods are just that – they neither stimulate nor calm and therefore can be eaten without harm, although not in excess or you will create another kind of imbalance.

All foods are changed by the way in which they are cooked. For example, methods which make food yang are frying, roasting, grilling, smoking and adding a lot of spice. On the other hand, yin methods of cooking are steaming, boiling and stewing. A neutral potato can be roasted into a yang food, or boiled into a yin food. Therefore, the wise diner takes this into account when he orders his meal.

Most established Chinese dishes are already harmonized in terms of ingredients, which is why they appear on so many menus. For example, the Hong Kong Chinese love to eat fresh crabs. In fact, in the autumn they are willing to pay for fresh crabs to be flown in from a particular area outside Shanghai to make up crab banquets, no expense spared. Crab, however, is a very yin food which by itself causes the body to be yin. Therefore, the chef always adds a herb known in Chinese as *Tzu-su*, or Purple Perilla in English. This tiny purplish herb is very stimulating and it balances out the effect of the crab meat. Without it, a person who is already yin would get a stomach ache or diarrhoea if he ate the crabs. Many Chinese also drink *Fa Diu*, a wine which neutralizes the yin of the crab.

Another interesting recipe frequently used by the southern Chinese is a special broth made for women who have just given birth. The broth is made from pig's knuckles, sweet vinegar, ginger and some hard-boiled eggs. It is ideal, as a woman who has just had a child suffers a calcium loss and the pig's knuckles supply calcium. The vinegar has several purposes – it dissolves the bone and makes it easier for the woman to absorb the calcium, it dilates the blood vessels and improves circulation, it helps the uterus to return to normal and expell any occult blood left behind and it stimulates the liver to produce bile which improves digestion. The ginger offsets any tendency to chill following the excess of sweating that accompanies labour. The meat and eggs provide protein.

A Chinese banquet closely follows the doctrine of harmony and is worth looking at as an example. Most begin either with something pickled, in the case of Shanghainese food, or something like sweet and sour pork. The vinegar in these dishes stimulates the liver and acts as an appetizer. This would be followed by some calming food, like vegetable dishes, which will prepare the stomach gently for the fun ahead. Then comes the yang dishes – meat in the form of chicken, duck, goose, beef or pork, roasted or deep-fried. After which is likely to be the shark's fin soup, with small dishes of vinegar which will help to dissolve the calcium in the shark's fin. Something fried follows – fried oysters or fish or shrimps – in order to neutralize the wetness of the soup and to avoid humidity in the body. To neutralize the fried food, the diners will move to a dish with vegetables, for example, celery and chicken.

Then will come the major fish dish – usually a large white fish like a pomfret or garoupa, steamed with ginger, scallions and coriander, which get rid of parasites, reduce the smell of the fish, clean the blood and supply vitamin C. Mushroom soup comes after this, with the mushrooms acting to clean out cholesterol left behind by any of the previous dishes. Next to last are the fried rice and noodles, to take up any remaining space. A sweet dish neutralizes the fried rice and noodles, and that is that – a perfectly balanced feast. Of course, each diner would have chosen the tea essential for his own balance that evening, whether stimulating or cooling.

The other thing that all diners take into account is the season of the year. The Chinese believe that it is unhealthy to eat foods out of their season and they consider many of the health problems of the West to be due to the effect on the body of constantly eating foods out of season. As a rough guideline, tradition suggests that food eaten in the spring should be stimulating and neutral. It should contain a balance of meats and vegetables, prepared in various ways. The weather is very changeable in the spring, and it is also the time when there is a lot of sickness about – a view confirmed by medical statistics in the West. The wise person therefore eats a variety of foods cooked in a variety of ways in order that he will not be caught out by sudden changes in the weather, but will already be following a mixed diet, neither too stimulating nor too cooling.

In summer, as might be expected, calming and cooling foods should feature highly in the diet. It should include more vegetables and less meat, avoid oily or fatty dishes and all stimulating alcohols. Fruit is good, since it brings out the yin in the body and balances out the yangness of the summer heat. Since heat mist and summer rain are particularly associated with humidity, it is also good to eat diuretic foods which reduce humidity in the body, such as celery, watermelon and cucumber.

Autumn is, of course, cooler and therefore there should be a move back towards more meats, with vegetables and fruit still included, and also to foods which help to retain fluids in the body, like dates, figs, pears and honey. This ensures sufficient lubrication in the body during the dry autumnal weather.

Winter requires plenty of stimulating foods – more meat, more high-protein foods and even some alcohol. This richer diet gives the body more stamina to withstand the winter.

We do not propose to tell you exactly how much to eat, since that is a very individual matter, but we suggest that you follow some good Chinese habits in your eating. For example, most Chinese never eat meat in the quantities thought normal by Westerners. The more traditional Chinese find a steak repellent in its size and taste. Instead the bulk of any meal is carbohydrates in the form of rice or wheat bread, vegetables and small amounts of meat. There is not really a strong tradition of vegetarianism among the Chinese, since this does not fit in with the concept of balance, but meat is always chopped or finely sliced. They get plenty of bulk in their diet, either through the vegetables they eat – because they are lightly cooked to retain crispness – or through chewing and eating parts that we usually do not – fish bones, fish heads, duck heads, chicken's feet and so on. That is healthy on several counts – one is the delay it causes which allows the stomach to send up messages of fullness to the brain. This means that the diner does not over-eat, which is what happens if every morsel of food slips quickly down. There is a time delay which can result in the diner eating more, thinking he is still hungry, when in fact it is only that the neuro system has not yet transmitted the full-up message. Secondly, it gives exercise to teeth and gums, which are massaged in the course of such chewing. Thirdly, and this is certainly not the least advantage, it provides plenty of fibre for the digestive system to work on.

Most Chinese eat several times a day, normally four or five at least. Some of these meals are no more than a bowl of noodles with a touch of vegetables, but it means a healthier digestive system and prevents the kind of hunger which then results in over-eating. Fatness is unusual among the southern Chinese and much of this may well be due to this habit of eating little and often. The latest research in the West suggests that people who eat more frequently may successfully diet by increasing the number of meals, while reducing their content.

Traditionally, the Chinese do not particularly like sugar or sweet things. It does not form a great part of their diet, although unfortunately some young Chinese have caught the Western addiction to sugar in forms like ice cream, chocolate and sweet cake. There were never many sweet dishes included in the Chinese diet, other than as tiny pastries to cleanse the palate between the courses of a banquet. Sweets mostly took the form of preserved fruit and nuts and many of these were sour rather than sweet. Also, another traditional habit was restraint when it came to alcohol. Although one of the most famous poets in Chinese history, Li Po, was a renowned drunkard, he was something of an exception. In the past, women seldom took alcohol and many men did not either. The correct accompaniment to most meals was tea, and hot tea at that. The Chinese consider it extremely unhealthy to take cold drinks, especially with food. It inhibits the digestion from doing its job properly and cold drinks taken by themselves cause severe shock to the body. It is far better, even on a hot day, to take a warm drink and many Chinese today prefer to drink plain hot water. In Hong Kong, young people like to drink hot Coca-Cola with lemon.

Adult Chinese seldom drank milk and even today there are many people who cannot digest milk. The enzyme which breaks down milk lives in the stomach only as long as it is needed. If a child is weaned off milk and does not drink it any more, he will later be unable to drink it without developing stomach pains, belching, diarrhoea or nausea. Although this was undoubtedly historically partly due to lack of milk, since animals were seldom kept for their milk, it is also a dietary habit. Milk and dairy products are still not often on the diet of middle-aged and old Chinese people, and the Chinese doctor would always suggest keeping dairy products to a minimum. They cause phlegm to build up throughout the body, starting with the nose and throat. The fact that many Americans now have allergies to milk and other dairy products is because they have been following an unnatural diet. The human body simply cannot cope with large amounts of dairy products and was not constructed to do so. They also build up cholesterol deposits in the blood vessels.

In summary, the Chinese eat little meat, plenty of vegetables, a reasonable amount of carbohydrates, little sugar, few dairy products and they take all this in several small meals a day, eating until their stomachs are 75 per cent full. Their diet is big in fibre, their vegetables are always undercooked and they do not take iced drinks.

In the section which follows you will find a list of common foods fairly typical of the average Western diet – with one or two slightly exotic additions when we feel that they are particularly valuable foods – analysed according to the Chinese system of categorizing food and drink. We list them alphabetically – for easy reference – and indicate whether they are stimulating, calming or neutral, also explaining how they affect the body and its workings. Assuming that it would also be helpful to start with a list of such items also categorized under the headings stimulating, calming and neutral, we have done that too. This will enable someone to devise a diet for himself along yin or calming, yang or stimulating and neutral guidelines. This means that anyone who wants to replace the items we suggest for the fourteen-day yin and the fourteen-day yang diets can do it easily by merely referring to the yin or yang items which will start our listing.

The reader will notice that we do not advocate a vegetarian diet. While we do recognize that many people feel that it is entirely valid for human beings to be vegetarian, or indeed that it is positively desirable, our concern at this stage is to educate people in general about all the aspects of their normal diet. In fact, many of the attributes of typical vegetarians – the philosophical concern with basic values, the spiritual aspects of their lives, their unaggressive approach to life – are also typically yin attributes. The aim of the very yin diet is to produce a person more inward-looking, more concerned with spiritual values and better fitted for a meditative life. This is why the Chinese religious life is so often concerned with keeping to a vegetarian diet. We feel that the person who wants to pursue such ideals will do so and will certainly already have a greater awareness of how food affects the body and the mind. On the other hand we would also like to bring good body, mind and spirit awareness into the daily lives of many people who perhaps are not very concerned with it and therefore do not realize how their eating affects them. Therefore we choose to deal with the whole range of average human eating and drinking.

In that category we do not include many of the features of the modern diet which induce such a state of imbalance that no one can really include them regularly in his eating regime and hope to live a balanced life. Among the items we exclude are commercial sugar-laden soft drinks, most commercial snack items, most commercial sweets and chocolates. We also exclude all items which are tinned, processed, smoked, preserved, crystallized, salted, pickled and commercially altered for packing, quick-cooking and convenience. We recognize that, for many reasons, people do use such items but they form no part of a natural and healthy diet. Therefore we make no further comment on them.

Neither do we deal with such Western concepts as calories, vitamins, proteins and other non-Chinese ways of categorizing foods. It is a way of looking at food which simply is not relevant to the Chinese. No doubt it is interesting to know the calorific value of a food item, but the Chinese do not feel that knowing that has anything to do with understanding how such food really affects the functioning of the body. Moreover, Chinese medical practitioners feel that most people would not have digestive or obesity problems if they ate foods which were properly processed by their bodies, and that depends upon the functioning of the body, not upon the protein value of the food.

Stimulating foods

All the foods and drinks listed here are stimulating, heating and yang:

apricots, barley, beef, black tea, carp, celery, cherries, chestnuts, chicken, chilli, coconut, cod, coriander, freshwater eel, garlic, ginger, goose, grapes, lamb, oats, olives, onions, oolong tea, pepper, pigeon, pineapple, plums, shrimps, squid, sugar, venison, vinegar, walnuts, wine.

Calming foods

All the foods and drinks listed here are calming, cooling and yin:

abalone, banana, beer, broad beans, mung beans, soya beans, beancurd, crab, cucumber, duck, eggplant (aubergine), frog's legs, kelp, lettuce, marrow, mulberries, mushrooms (button), oranges,

> oysters, pears, peas, persimmons, pumpkins, rabbit, rock salt, snails, spinach, sugar cane, sunflower seeds, tangerines, green tea, tomatoes, watercress, watermelon, wheat.

Neutral foods

All the following foods and drinks are neutral. They are neither yin nor yang and do not change the diet in any way. Therefore, they can be added to either a stimulating or a calming dish without altering the balance of the meal.

They include:

> apples, cabbage, carrots, catfish, cauliflower, clams, saltwater eel, figs, guava, honey, milk, Chinese black mushrooms, papaya, peanuts, perch, pork, potatoes, quail, rice, black sesame seeds, sweet corn, taro, yoghurt.

Although all the above are neutral, this does not mean they do not affect the organs of the body. In fact, several of them are powerful and all of them have some effect on at least one body organ. They are only neutral in their effect on the yin or yang balance of the body. For their actual effect on body organs, see the full alphabetical listing which follows:

Toxic foods

These are items which are considered to be slightly toxic. They are often associated with allergic reactions, both among the Chinese and in the West. It does not mean they should be excluded from the diet, since they are all powerful foods. However, some people may actually have allergic reactions on eating any amount of these foods, however small, while other people will experience such reactions only if they eat them to excess.

Among the toxic foods are:

> apricots, garlic, goose, pineapple, green or sprouting potatoes, shrimps.

Other foods which may be toxic to certain people with certain conditions are itemized in the alphabetical list. When devising a diet for yourself, check every item before including it and pay heed to the warnings appended to certain items.

ABALONE calming

Affects: liver and lungs

Action: Regulates liver functions, improves vision, stops thirst and relieves feelings of heat in the body
It cools yang-excess liver conditions, alleviates dizziness, hypertension and lymph gland swellings

APPLE neutral

Affects: spleen and stomach

Action: Nourishes the heart, stops thirst and increases saliva, lubricates the lungs and cuts down phlegm
It balances out the deficiencies of the digestive system and aids digestion, alleviates constipation and hypertension

APRICOT stimulating

Affects: liver, heart and stomach

Action: Relieves coughing and lubricates the lungs, stops thirst and increases saliva
It stimulates the appetite

Warning: Those who suffer from boils, skin problems and eczema should not eat apricots since they are somewhat toxic. Pregnant women should not eat them either

AUBERGINE see Eggplant

BANANA calming

Affects: lungs and large intestine

Action: Lubricates and cools the lungs, eases restlessness, is a mild laxative, improves blood circulation, alleviates hypertension and alcohol intoxication
It cools over-heated bowels, alleviates coughing and bleeding haemorrhoids

Warning: Those who have chronic diarrhoea or suffer from deficient conditions of the stomach and large intestine should not eat bananas

BARLEY stimulating

Affects: Liver and spleen by nourishing the spleen and stomach and by regulating imbalanced liver functions

Action: It alleviates indigestion and promotes appetite. Barley sprouts will help a nursing mother to produce more milk

BEAN, broad calming

Affects: lungs and large intestine

Action: Helps blood to coagulate, lowers blood pressure and acts as a diuretic
It is useful in cases of blood in the stool and alleviates hypertension

Warning: People with deficient stomachs, indigestion and G6PD (a rare blood condition) must not eat this

BEAN, French neutral

Affects: spleen and stomach by regulating their functions

Action: Drives humidity from the body, alleviates diarrhoea and vomiting

It also helps to control restlessness and coughing

It is effective against leucorrhoea

Warning: People suffering from deficient stomachs should not eat French beans

BEAN, mung calming

Affects: heart, liver and stomach

Action: Acts as a detoxifying agent and diuretic, reduces body heat and calms restlessness

It alleviates urinary retention, reduces swelling in the feet and legs and is good for acne, boils and sores

Warning: People suffering from conditions associated with deficiencies in the spleen, stomach or kidneys should not eat mung beans. (Most beansprouts in Chinese restaurants are mung beansprouts)

BEAN, soya calming

Affects: lungs

Action: Relieves feelings of heat in the body, alleviates restlessness and helps minor burns and insect bites to heal

BEANCURD (tofu) calming

Affects: lungs and large intestine

Action: Calms the body, alleviates chest conditions, acts as a diuretic and removes congestion in the large intestine
It is helpful in cases of blood in the stool, leg ulcers and burns

BEEF stimulating

Affects: stomach and spleen

Action: It nourishes the spleen, tonifies the stomach and helps to build healthy bones and tendons
It is effective in strengthening a weak stomach and spleen, reduces swelling, eases lower-back pain and alleviates anaemia

Warning: Those suffering from dermatitis, skin diseases, cancer, hepatitis and rhinitis should not eat beef

BUCKWHEAT neutral

Affects: spleen and stomach by improving the functions of the stomach

Action: It relaxes the intestines and helps to reduce blood pressure
It can be useful to cool an excess-yang stomach, to alleviate diarrhoea caused by intestinal problems and to counteract cold sweating

CABBAGE neutral

Affects: stomach

Action: Acts as a pain reliever

CARP stimulating

Affects spleen, lungs, liver and kidneys

Action: It relieves humidity in the body and acts as a diuretic, relieving oedema

It stabilizes the foetus in the womb and improves lactation in nursing mothers. It also alleviates coughing and asthma

Warning: People suffering from skin infections, boils, sores, septic spots and ulcers should not eat carp

CARROT neutral

Affects: spleen, stomach and lungs

Action: It relieves congestion in the chest and cools body heat, acting as a detoxifying agent throughout the body

It is very useful since it can be combined successfully with many other foods

CATFISH neutral

Affects: spleen and kidneys by nourishing the blood, tonifying the kidneys and regulating the functions of the spleen and stomach

Actions: It eases arthritic, lower-back and knee-joint pains. It also alleviates nosebleeds and ringing in the ears

CAULIFLOWER neutral

Affects: stomach and spleen by regulating the functions of both

Actions: It alleviates indigestion

CELERY stimulating

Affects: lungs, stomach and kidneys by tonifying the spleen and stomach and regulating the functions of the kidneys

Action: It alleviates hypertension, mild diabetes, insomnia, coughing and headaches
In cases of excessive bleeding after childbirth, it can bring relief as it helps blood to clot. For the same reason, it is useful in cases of blood in the urine

Warning: While celery is an excellent food for yin people, yang people should avoid it

CHEESE neutral

Affects: stomach, spleen and lungs

Action: Lubricates and nourishes the spleen and lungs, tonifies the stomach and relieves stomach pain
It is good for physical weakness, mild stomach pains and eases constipation

CHERRY stimulating

Affects: liver, stomach and kidneys, by regulating the functions of the stomach and nourishing the spleen

Action: Improves the appetite and alleviates thirst and diarrhoea

Warning: Those who have physical injuries or suffer from nausea, boils or sores should not eat cherries

CHESTNUT stimulating

Affects: spleen and stomach and nourishes the kidneys

Action: It is helpful for those who have arthritis or suffer from weakness in the lower back and legs and alleviates bronchitis

CHICKEN stimulating

Affects: liver, spleen and stomach

Action: It relieves rheumatic pain, helps general physical debility and tonifies blood and *chi*

CHILLI stimulating

Affects: spleen, stomach, liver and large intestine

Action: By stimulating the stomach, chilli relieves indigestion, promotes appetite and strengthens a weak stomach

Warning: People suffering from any of the following should not eat chilli: inflamed eyes, hepatitis, rhinitis, haemorrhoids and sore throat

CLAM neutral

Affects: lungs, liver and spleen

Action: Reduces phlegm, acts as an antacid in the stomach and promotes urination

COCONUT stimulating

Affects: lungs and heart

Action: It quenches thirst, relieves swelling and kills tapeworms

COD stimulating

Affects: spleen, stomach, liver and lungs

Action: It regulates the functions of the spleen and stomach, tonifies the liver and lubricates the lungs

It improves vision and is excellent for weak, deficient stomachs. It alleviates night blindness and improves dry skin

CORIANDER stimulating (mild)

Affects: heart, spleen and stomach

Action: It improves circulation and digestion and alleviates both hypertension and indigestion

Warning: Do not eat excessive amounts of coriander since it causes damage to the eyes

CRAB cool

Affects: liver and stomach

Action: Improves the digestion and regulates the functions of the stomach. It improves blood circulation and relieves feelings of heat in the body

It is good for people suffering from physical injuries and for women with abdominal pains after childbirth

Warning: Crab must never be eaten together with persimmon (in a good Chinese restaurant, sweet and sour sauce is made from persimmon)

People suffering from the following conditions must not eat crabs: skin diseases, eczema, rashes, boils, dermatitis and skin allergies

CUCUMBER calming

Affects: stomach and small intestine

Action: It cools body heat, relieves thirst and acts as a diuretic. It can help to cool a fever, to alleviate restlessness and urinary retention

Warning: People suffering from the following conditions should not eat cucumber: skin diseases, sores, boils, rashes, itching, swollen feet

DUCK calming

Affects: lungs and kidneys

Action: Nourishes the blood and sedates the body. It can act as a diuretic and, in cases of oedema due to kidney deficiency, it can alleviate the condition

It is also effective in cases of anaemia, insomnia and nervousness

Warning: Only ducks of three years old and over have medicinal value

Those suffering from the following conditions should not eat duck: skin infections, rashes, ringworm, boils, sores, ulcers and influenza

EGGS stimulating

Affects: lungs, kidneys, spleen and stomach

Action: This is good for both kidney yin and kidney yang conditions, since it affects the adrenal glands and stimulates hormone production (only in the case of fertilized eggs, of course). It also tonifies the blood, the stomach and spleen

It is good for anaemia, diarrhoea, cases of nervous breakdown or mental agitation, and can be effective in cases of sexual deficiency due to kidney *chi* deficiency. It is helpful in cases of infertility, impotence or frigidity

EEL (freshwater) stimulating

Affects: spleen and kidneys

Action: It tonifies the spleen and relieves rheumatic pain, alleviates haemorrhoids and prolapse of the anus
It is also helpful in mild cases of diabetes

EEL (saltwater) neutral

Affects: spleen, lungs and kidneys

Action: It relieves rheumatic pain, nourishes the whole body, tonifies the lungs and kills roundworms
It is excellent for general weakness, coughing and swelling of the lymph glands

EGGPLANT (aubergine) calming

Affects: intestine and stomach

Action: Relieves stomach and intestinal pain, reduces bruising, relieves swelling and is also a diuretic. It relaxes tension in the intestines

Warning: Since the eggplant is extremely cooling, it should be avoided by yin people and those suffering from deficient conditions

FIG neutral

Affects: lungs, spleen and stomach

Action: Lubricates and cools the lungs, lubricates the large intestine and improves the appetite. It kills roundworms and pinworms and alleviates sore throats, laryngitis, dry coughing, indigestion, constipation, haemorrhoids and prolapse of the anus

FROG'S LEGS calming

Affects: spleen and stomach

Action: It tonifies the stomach, detoxifies the system and is a diuretic
It alleviates malaria, irregular menstruation and relieves swelling

GARLIC stimulating

Affects: spleen and kidneys

Action: It removes humidity from the body, warms up the spleen and the stomach, kills parasites, relieves indigestion and improves the digestive functions
It is also good for cleaning the body
It alleviates boils, sores, swellings, diarrhoea and abdominal pain

Warning: Garlic is slightly toxic and therefore should not be eaten to excess, since this damages the spleen, lungs and eyes and causes excess sputum and coughing
Yang people suffering from yin-deficient conditions should avoid garlic, as should those who have yang-excess livers

GINGER stimulating

Affects: lungs, spleen and stomach

Action: Relieves cold, acts as a diuretic, stops vomiting, tonifies the stomach and improves the appetite

It also helps to clear toxins out of the body in cases where food poisoning due to bad meat has occurred

GOOSE stimulating

Affects: stomach and spleen

Action: It is generally tonifying, regulating the stomach and balancing its deficiencies

Warning: Since goose is slightly toxic, those suffering from the following conditions should not eat it: skin diseases, sores, boils, itching, rashes, eczema and cancer

GRAPE stimulating

Affects: spleen and liver, by nourishing the blood and tonifying the stomach and spleen

Action: It alleviates restlessness, acts as a diuretic and helps to relieve rheumatism

Warning: Those suffering from diabetes and chronic constipation should not eat grapes

GUAVA neutral

Affects: spleen, kidneys and large intestine

Action: It eases stomach pains and diarrhoea

Warning: Those suffering from chronic constipation should not eat guava

HARE see Rabbit

HAWTHORN BERRIES calming

Affects: spleen and stomach

Action: Relieves indigestion, clears bruising, lowers blood pressure, improves circulation and lowers cholesterol

This is good for hypertension and the early stages of dysentery

Warning: People with weak stomachs should not eat the berries and no one should eat them with stimulating foods

HONEY neutral

Affects: lungs, spleen and large intestine, by lubricating the lungs and tonifying a weak spleen and stomach. It nourishes the spleen

Action: It is good for the complexion and clears it of blemishes. It alleviates constipation and helps mouth ulcers and burns to heal

Warning: People with diarrhoea should not eat honey

KELP calming

Affects: liver and stomach

Action: It is a diuretic, alleviates mild hernia cases and eases hypertension

LAMB stimulating

Affects: spleen, stomach and kidneys; tonifies blood and *chi* and nourishes the kidneys

Action: Improves the appetite, increases body stamina and helps general debility

It eases lower-back pain, alleviates impotence, chilliness in the body, fatigue and anaemia

Warning: It should not be eaten by those suffering from the following conditions: fever, common cold, influenza, toothache. Excess-yang types should also avoid eating lamb

LETTUCE calming

Affects: stomach and intestines, improving the functions of the stomach

Action: It relieves body heat and acts as a diuretic

MANGO cooling

Affects: liver, spleen and stomach

Action: Since this is regarded as a somewhat toxic food it is not used for any food therapy

Warning: Those suffering from swellings, deficiencies of spleen and stomach or rheumatism should not eat mangoes

MARROW calming

Affects: lungs, spleen – in particular the pancreas – and the intestines

Action: It is a diuretic and it prevents thirst, alleviates irritability and detoxifies the body after it has been affected by food poisoning due to bad fish

It also helps people suffering from the following conditions: boils, sores, urinary retention, hot flushes, abdominal distention and diabetes

If you want to lose weight, eat marrow cooked with the skin left on

Warning: Do not eat marrow with tonifying or stimulating foods. If you are yin-deficient, do not eat marrow at all

MILK neutral

Affects: lungs and stomach

Action: Tonifies the stomach and lungs and lubricates the lungs and intestines
It is good for weak stomachs, increases saliva and alleviates constipation

Warning: Do not drink milk if you suffer from a very cold stomach or diarrhoea

MULBERRY calming

Affects: lungs, liver, kidneys and large intestine

Action: Stops thirst, acts as both a diuretic and a laxative, lubricates the lungs and nourishes the liver and blood
It alleviates restlessness, coughing and chronic constipation

MUSHROOM (Chinese black) neutral

Affects: liver and stomach, improving the function of the stomach

Action: Lowers blood pressure, reduces cholesterol and helps to prevent cancer

MUSHROOMS (white) calming (mild)

Affects: liver and stomach, improving the stomach functions

Action: Alleviates diarrhoea and phlegm, helps to prevent cancer and acts as a detoxifying agent in the body. It can also be a help in cases of hepatitis

OAT stimulating

Affects: lungs, spleen and stomach

Action: Nourishes the lungs, reduces cholesterol and generally tonifies the system
It is good for those suffering from bronchitis, tuberculosis and general debility

OLIVE stimulating

Affects: lungs and stomach

Action: Improves the appetite, relieves sore throats, acts as a detoxifying agent, especially in cases of shellfish poisoning, and alleviates drunkenness

Warning: People with weak or deficient stomachs should not eat olives

ONION (large white, red or Spanish) stimulating

Affects: lungs, spleen, liver and intestine

Action: It heats the organs, thus stimulating their functions and improves blood circulation
It is helpful in cases of the common cold, influenza, diarrhoea and parasites (especially worms). It also heats a cold stomach, one sign of which can be diarrhoea

Warning: People who are yang excess should not eat onions, especially if they are suffering from a yang excess of the kidneys and stomach

ONION, spring stimulating

Affects: lungs, liver and stomach

Action: Relaxes the muscles, induces perspiration, improves the functions of the lungs, detoxifies the body and reduces swelling

It alleviates the following conditions: common cold, headaches, fever, nasal congestion, swollen face, sluggish urination, sluggish bowels and bladder, diarrhoea and vomiting

It can help to relieve milk retention in nursing mothers, and it is also very useful to help to restore normal functioning to the body after food poisoning, as it speeds up the detoxification process

The medicinal part of the plant is centred around the white stalk and the roots, not in the green stem

Warning: Those who sweat excessively should avoid eating spring onions, as should people suffering yin-deficient conditions with fever

ORANGE calming

Affects: stomach, large and small intestine

Action: Stops bleeding, is diuretic and acts as a mild laxative

It alleviates nausea, constipation and bleeding haemorrhoids

OYSTER calming

Affects: liver and kidneys

Action: Alleviates swelling of the lymph glands, reduces phlegm, nourishes the blood, tranquillizes the body and reduces swelling

It is also good for nervous tension and alleviates dizziness, excessive sweating and nocturnal emissions

PAPAYA neutral

Affects: spleen, heart, lungs and liver

Action: It nourishes the spleen and stomach and therefore improves digestion, lubricates the lungs and therefore helps coughing
It also alleviates the following conditions: stomach pains, indigestion, eczema, boils and sores
It helps to promote lactation in nursing mothers

PEA calming (mild)

Affects: heart, spleen, stomach and large intestine

Action: Acts as a diuretic, alleviates diarrhoea and hiccoughing, and is a detoxifying agent in the body
It also promotes urination, counteracts distention of the abdomen and alleviates diabetes

PEANUT neutral

Affects: lungs and spleen, by lubricating the lungs and stimulating the spleen

Action: Improves the appetite, regulates the blood and acts as a diuretic
It alleviates swellings and blood in the urine, and helps the flow of the nursing mother's milk
Peanuts should be boiled, steamed or

made into a soup. Roasted or fried, they are too stimulating

PEAR calming

Affects: heart, lungs and stomach

Action: Lubricates the lungs and stops thirst, acts as a diuretic, relieves restlessness, reduces body heat, detoxifies the body, alleviates coughing and phlegm in hot and yang-excess people

It helps the following conditions: loss of voice, red painful eyes, sluggish bladder and bowels, alcoholic poisoning

Warning: Anyone suffering from cold deficient stomach, chronic diarrhoea or anaemia in pregnancy should not eat pears

Only yang-excess people should eat pears

PEPPER stimulating

Affects: lungs, stomach and large intestine by warming and stimulating the lungs and stomach

Action: It alleviates the common cold, balances a deficient stomach, eases indigestion and a phlegmatic cough

Warning: People suffering from yang-excess conditions should not use pepper

PERCH neutral

Affects: spleen, stomach, liver and kidneys

Action: Tonifies spleen and stomach, nourishes liver and kidneys

It improves the appetite, stimulates

sluggish urination and alleviates physical weakness

PERSIMMON calming

Affects: spleen, lungs and large intestine

Action: Lubricates the lungs and relieves coughing, reduces phlegm, stops diarrhoea and nourishes the spleen

It can help the following conditions: burning sore throat, dry mouth and hypertension

Warning: Never eat persimmon together with crab

People suffering from anaemia, influenza and the common cold should not eat persimmon

PIGEON stimulating

Affects: lungs and kidneys

Action: Tonifies blood and *chi*, removes humidity from the body, warms the entire body

It is good for general physical weakness, irregular menstruation, impotence, skin sores and itchiness

PINEAPPLE stimulating

Affects: lungs and large intestine

Action: Relieves discomfort caused by summer heat, alleviates indigestion and diarrhoea

It helps in cases of sunstroke and restlessness

Warning: Pineapple is slightly toxic and therefore some people are allergic to it

Signs of this allergy are vomiting, stomach pains, diarrhoea, headache, dizziness, itchy skin, numbness in the tongue
The Chinese usually put slices of pineapple in salt water to wash it and reduce its toxicity

PLUM stimulating (mild)
Affects: liver and stomach
Action: Improves appetite, relieves indigestion, stops thirst and increases saliva, regulates the liver function
It is also used in cases of sluggish urination, liver sclerosis and constipation
Warning: People suffering from excess phlegm and weak stomachs should not eat plums

PORK neutral
Affects: spleen and kidneys
Action: Nourishes the internal organs and lubricates the skin
It helps to counteract loss of weight and alleviates general debility
Warning: People subject to obesity should not eat pork, nor anyone suffering from excess phlegm

POTATO neutral
Affects: stomach and large intestine by tonifying the stomach and spleen
Action: Regulates the functions of the digestive system
It alleviates constipation and stomach

pains. Applied externally, it can be used in cases of eczema

Warning: Never eat potatoes that are green or have shoots on, as these are toxic

PUMPKIN calming

Affects: stomach and large intestine

Action: Removes humidity from the body, kills worms, relieves fever, stops diarrhoea and also helps to stabilize the foetus in the womb

It alleviates leg ulcers and eczema on the scrotum

Warning: Do not eat pumpkin to excess, as it will make your skin somewhat yellow

QUAIL neutral

Affects: lungs and spleen

Action: Regulates the functions of spleen and stomach, relieves swelling and acts as a diuretic

It also helps the following conditions: poor appetite, indigestion, malnutrition and bronchial asthma

RABBIT calming

Affects: spleen

Action: Tonifies the spleen, nourishes the blood, stops thirst and lubricates the large intestine

It alleviates the following conditions: anaemia, insomnia, bed-wetting and weight loss

RICE neutral

Affects: spleen and stomach by tonifying them
Action: Eases restlessness and stops diarrhoea

SALT, rock calming

Affects: lungs, stomach and kidneys
Action: Both diuretic and laxative. It reduces body heat, clears phlegm and alleviates the following conditions: sore throats, toothache and constipation
Warning: It should not be taken by people suffering from the following conditions: kidney diseases, oedema, asthma and hypertension

SESAME SEEDS, black neutral

Affects: lungs, spleen, large intestine and kidneys
Action: Acts as a mild laxative, nourishes the lungs, increases body energy, helps to improve blood circulation and lubricates the skin
It alleviates constipation and urinary retention and helps to prevent hair loss
Warning: People suffering from the following conditions should not eat black sesame seeds: diarrhoea, toothache, dermatitis and boils

SHRIMP stimulating

Affects: liver and lungs
Action: Tonifies the kidneys, improves lactation in nursing mothers and reduces phlegm, It also helps in cases of impotence
Warning: Due to the slightly toxic nature of

shrimps, people suffering from the following conditions should not eat them: skin diseases, dermatitis, eczema, rashes, sores, boils, skin allergies, skin cancer, sepsis, ear infection and haemorrhoids

SNAIL calming

Affects: spleen, kidneys and large intestine

Action: Removes humidity from the body, detoxifies and clears heat from the body, acts as a diuretic, relieves drunkenness and improves lactation in nursing mothers
It is good for the following conditions: inflamed eyes, sluggish urination, diabetes and alcoholic intoxication

Warning: People with cold or deficient stomachs should not eat snails

SPINACH calming

Affects: large and small intestines, stomach and bladder

Action: Improves the gastro-intestinal functions, relieves tightness of the chest, cools excess heat in the stomach and intestines, eases retention of urine, cleans the body after alcoholic poisoning

Warning: People with cold, weak and deficient stomachs should not eat spinach

Note: If spinach is well cooked, this reduces the cooling effect that it has on the body. Taken raw, under-cooked or in soup, it has a laxative and diuretic effect

SQUASH see Pumpkin

SQUID stimulating (mild)
Affects: liver and kidneys
Action: Nourishes the blood and tonifies the stomach
It alleviates the following conditions: irregular menstruation, anaemia and hyperacidity of the stomach

SUGAR, light and dark brown, raw stimulating
Affects: liver and spleen, by regulating their functions. It also lubricates the lungs
Action: Good for the following conditions: pharyngitis, thirst and dry coughing
Warning: People suffering from diabetes, excess phlegm and tooth decay should not eat sugar

SUGAR CANE calming
Affects: lungs, spleen and stomach
Action: Stops thirst, lubricates the large and small intestines and nourishes the liver
It alleviates constipation
Warning: People with diabetes or cold or deficient stomachs should not eat sugar cane

SUNFLOWER SEED calming
Affects: liver, lungs and kidneys, by regulating the liver and lubricating the lungs
Action: Removes humidity from the body, acts as a diuretic and kills worms
It alleviates the following conditions: dizziness, hypertension, inflammation of the prostate gland and urinary retention

SWEET CORN neutral

Affects: stomach and kidneys
Action: Regulates the function of the gall bladder, alleviates hypertension and acts as a diuretic

TANGERINE calming

Affects: lungs and stomach
Action: Clears the stomach, activates the intestines, is a diuretic and increases saliva
It cools a hot stomach
Warning: It is not good for people with deficient stomachs and lungs or chronic diarrhoea

TARO neutral

Affects: spleen and stomach by improving their function
Action: It can be applied raw, externally, to relieve pain, swelling and inflammation
Eaten, it alleviates swelling of the lymph glands
Warning: People suffering from stomach ulcers should not eat taro
Eating excess amounts of it causes indigestion

TEA, green calming (mild)

Affects: heart, spleen, kidneys and large intestine
Action: Increases saliva, stops thirst, improves digestion, acts as a diuretic, refreshes the body, clears heat from the body and reduces fat
It is good for the following conditions: restlessness, sluggish urination, indigestion and high cholesterol

Warning: Green tea should not be drunk when you are tired or fatigued, nor should you combine it with the taking of medicine or ginseng

TOFU see Beancurd

TOMATO calming

Affects: liver, spleen and stomach, by regulating the liver and tonifying the stomach

Action: Detoxifies the body, relieves indigestion and cools the blood

Note: It is excellent for yang people and those suffering yang-excess conditions

Warning: Yin people or those suffering from deficient conditions should not eat tomatoes

VENISON stimulating

Affects: kidneys

Action: Tonifies the kidneys and nourishes bone and bone marrow

It alleviates the following conditions: lower-back pain, premature ejaculation, impotence, and milk congestion in nursing mothers

VINEGAR, rice or cider or wine stimulating

Affects: liver

Action: Relieves swelling, improves the circulation of the blood, heals bruises and helps indigestion

Warning: People suffering from muscle cramps, cavities in their teeth and peptic ulcers should not take vinegar

Note: Always take vinegar from utensils made of glass, porcelain or earthenware. Plastic or metals leech into the liquid and cause imbalances in the body

WALNUT stimulating

Affects: lungs, kidneys and liver by lubricating the lungs and large intestine and nourishing the kidneys

Action: It alleviates the following conditions: kidney deficiencies, frequency of urination, lower-back pain, weakness in the legs, nocturnal emission and impotence

Warning: People suffering from the following conditions should not eat walnuts: diarrhoea, indigestion, colds and influenza
Eating excessive amounts of walnuts can cause nausea and vomiting

WATERCRESS calming (mild)

Affects: lungs by calming, cooling and lubricating them

Action: Alleviates sore throats, irritability and dry coughing

Warning: It should not be taken by those with yin stomachs and lungs or with diarrhoea due to deficient conditions

WATERMELON calming

Affects: heart, lungs, spleen and kidneys

Action: Relieves summer heat, stops thirst, eases restlessness and acts as a diuretic
It alleviates sunstroke and mouth ulcers

Warning: Yin types with deficient stomachs and people suffering from stomach ulcers should not eat watermelon

WHEAT calming

Affects: spleen and stomach
Action: Alleviates high temperature and thirst and acts as a diuretic and tranquillizer

YOGHURT neutral

Affects: liver, stomach, lungs and large intestine
Action: Tonifies the stomach, lubricates the lungs and large intestine
It helps weak stomachs, constipation and sluggish bowels

Part Five

Common Ailments and Conditions

This section is exactly what the heading suggests – a list of the most common health problems which make people's lives less happy, less productive and therefore less balanced. Many of these ailments are the long-term persistent kind which the sufferer eventually comes to believe must always be a part of his existence, the kind which seldom respond to orthodox treatment. Others are what often appear to be isolated symptoms which, since they are not tied in with any other specific disease, do not really have any form of treatment within the normal confines of Western medicine. The reader will see from glancing through the section that there are a number of suggested ways of treating such symptoms simply by what we eat. In Chinese medicine, it is not necessary to have a specific illness to be considered in need of help. Any symptom of disharmony deserves attention because it indicates that all is not as it should be within the body. The Chinese traditional doctor believes that the individual knows his body better than any doctor and he knows when things are just not right, even though he does not have the medical knowledge to name his own disease.

We most certainly do not suggest that this list makes your doctor redundant. If you are ill, you are right to seek responsible medical help. That is as much part of your responsibility to yourself as is the food that you put in your mouth. However, the more self-aware you become, the healthier your lifestyle will be because you will develop into someone who is his own body's best friend. This list is intended to educate you about the use of our own most natural medicine – the food we eat every day – to act as a back-up to medical conditions already diagnosed and being treated by your own chosen medical practitioner, and also to alleviate the various symptoms mentioned here that you may occasionally suffer from.

You will see that the list is in alphabetical order, with occasional cross-references, for easy consultation. Often there may be more than one suggested food therapy available. In this case pick one that specially appeals to you and try it for a while. Move to another one if you find it does not seem to help, but do not expect overnight results. Your body took a long time to manifest its imbalance and, to become really healthy again it also needs time. Since all these forms of treatment only use ordinary food, you cannot come to harm with them, provided you heed any warnings given with the treatment.

Preparation of the medicines

We refer to all the treatments as medicines since that is what they are. This is not a recreational cookery book and you must not add anything other than the suggested ingredients, cooked exactly according to the instructions given, neither must you change the cooking method. The making of medicinal food bears no relationship to ordinary Chinese cooking. You will notice that many of the medicines require continuous boiling for a long period of time, and this is in order that the effective ingredient in the food is extracted into the liquid which you will drink.

When the medicine is to be taken several times a day, the instructions usually refer to the total amount which you must make and which you must then drink, or eat, in proportionate doses. Put the remainder into a vacuum flask to keep it warm. This is better than reheating, which is not considered to be so good. When the medicine is to be taken two or three times a week, make the amount stated and take it all in the one day. Then make fresh medicine on each additional day.

All ingredients must be as fresh as possible. Tinned, frozen or processed versions of any of these ingredients will not be as good. Where you cannot get fresh at all – in the case of some of the juices, for example – the product you get must be 100 per cent pure and unprocessed with nothing added. All additives and all chemical processes change the nature of the food we eat, usually by making it heating or stimulating. All meats should be fresh and untreated with drugs, not chilled or frozen. This is difficult since most meats are full of steroids and antibiotics, but shop around and try to get free-range meat and poultry.

While this section gives therapeutic food guidance, you should not ignore your other basic food needs which will be according to the type of person you are and any conditions you think you may have. You will find further guidance on those matters by reading the other sections in this book and by checking out the various tables appended to those sections.

Symptoms

ABDOMINAL distention:
Juice 75 g/3 oz fresh peas and drink the liquid.
Do this twice a day.

ABDOMINAL pain after childbirth:
Take 12 g/½ oz dried crab shell and grind it to powder;
mix with 25 ml/1 fl oz of rice wine and drink the mixture.
Do this twice daily.

ACNE:
Take 100 g/4 oz mung beans, 50 g/2 oz raw brown sugar;
boil all together in 900 ml/1½ pt of water until reduced to half.
Eat and drink the results.

ANAEMIA:
There are several suggested therapies. Choose one and stick with it until it works.
If you have given it a reasonable period of time – say, one month – and see no improvement, change your therapy. Do not combine them.

1. Take 125 g/5 oz minced beef, 2 slices fresh ginger;
   boil for 10 minutes in 450 ml/¾ pt water.

Eat and drink while the mixture is hot.
Do this once a day at bedtime.

2. Take 250 g/10 oz lamb, 25 g/1 oz fresh ginger, 25 g/1 oz garlic;
   boil in 1·2 l/2 pt water until reduced to 900 ml/1½ pt.
   Divide into 2 halves and eat 125 g/5 oz twice daily.
3. Take 2 kg/5 lb rabbit meat, 100 g/4 oz fresh ginger;
   boil in 1·8–2·4 l/3–4 pt water until reduced to 1·2 l/2 pt and allow to cool.
   Drink 125 ml/5 fl oz of the resulting soup 2 or 3 times daily.
4. Take 400 g/1 lb squid, 100 g/4 oz black beans, 12 g/½ oz fresh ginger, some salt;
   steam in 600 ml/1 pt water.
   Eat 150 g/6 oz twice daily.
   Continue this for 4 to 6 days.

APPETITE, poor:

There are several suggested therapies. Choose one and try it until improvement occurs, not changing it until one week is over.

1. Eat 100 g/4 oz fresh cherries twice daily or drink 100 ml/4 fl oz cherry juice before eating your main meals.
2. Eat 2 apricots 2 or 3 times a day or drink 100 ml/4 fl oz apricot juice 2 or 3 times a day.
3. Take 25 g/1 oz chilli (fresh or powder), 100 ml/4 fl oz vinegar (wine, cider or rice), 12 g/½ oz soy sauce;

mix them together.
Swallow 1 teaspoonful before and after meals.

4. Take 150 g/6 oz barley and 75 g/3 oz raw brown sugar:
   boil in 600 ml/1 pt water until reduced to half.
   Drink the liquid while still lukewarm.
5. Take 400 g/1 lb perch, 25 g/1 oz spring onions, 6 g/¼ oz fresh ginger, some salt, some soy sauce;
   steam until ready.
   Eat.
   Do this 3 times a week.

ARTERIOSCLEROSIS:

Take 75 g/3 oz kelp, 100 g/4 oz sliced raw beef;
boil in 600 ml/1 pt water until reduced by half.
Eat and drink the results.
Do this as often as you like.

ASTHMA:

Juice 125 g/5 oz fresh figs.
Drink once daily.

BACK, lower-back pain:

There are several suggested remedies, of which you should choose one and stick with it for a month. If there is not sufficient improvement, try another one.

1. Take 75 g/3 oz fresh walnuts and crush them;
   mix with 50 g/2 oz raw brown sugar and add to 150 ml/6 fl oz warmed wine.
   Drink 75–100 ml/3–4 fl oz once or twice daily.

2. Take 400 g/1 lb venison, 50 g/2 oz garlic, 25 g/1 oz ginger;
   boil in 1·5 l/2½ pt water until reduced to 900 ml/1½ pt.
   Divide the results into 3 and eat and drink 3 times in 1 week.
3. Take 100 g/4 oz mussels, 100 g/4 oz pork, 50 g/2 oz garlic, 100 g/4 oz potato;
   boil all together in 1·2 l/2 pt water until reduced to 600 ml/1 pt.
   Eat and drink once daily.
   Continue doing this for 6 to 12 days.

BACK, weakness in lower back:

Take 7 fresh chestnuts and dry them in an oven or under a grill, but do not brown them.
Eat them once or twice daily.
Continue doing this for 1 or 2 months.

BITE, scorpion:

Mash raw garlic and apply it to the bite. Also eat 2 to 4 cloves of garlic daily while the bite is troublesome.

BITE, snake (non-poisonous):

Mash some raw eggplant (aubergine) and apply it to the bite.

BLADDER, infection:

Take 75 g/3 oz of the silky threads which are attached to a corncob;
boil them in 600 ml/1 pt water until reduced by half.
Put the mixture into a vacuum flask and drink the liquid 4 or 5 times daily.

BLOOD, platelet insufficiency:

Take 12–25 g/½–1 oz red grape wine.
Drink 3 times daily.

BOIL:

There are two suggestions, the first of which will sting.

1. Mash raw garlic and apply it to the boil;
   at the same time, eat 3 to 4 cloves of garlic daily while the boil is still active.
2. Take 100 g/4 oz mung beans, 50 g/2 oz kelp, 75 g/3 oz raw brown sugar;
   boil all together in 1200 ml/2 pt water until reduced by half.
   Eat and drink the results in 3–4 portions throughout day.

BOWEL, sluggish:

There are two suggestions which could be combined.

1. Eat 150 g/6 oz yoghurt (must be live, with no artificial additives) for breakfast each day.
2. Drink 150 ml/6 fl oz fresh pear juice for breakfast each day.

BREATH, shortness of:

Take 400 g/1 lb salmon, 50 g/2 oz garlic, 6 g/¼ oz fresh ginger, some salt, some soy sauce;
place all flavourings over the salmon and steam.
Eat in 3 portions throughout 1 day.

BRONCHITIS:

Take 150 g/6 oz chestnuts and 125 g/5 oz pork;
braise them together.
Eat 3 or 4 oz twice daily.

BURN:

Apply fresh honey to the burn.

or

Mix 50 g/2 oz beancurd with 25 g/1 oz raw brown sugar and apply mixture to the burn.

CHILBLAINS:

Take 100 g/4 oz chilli (fresh or powder);
boil in 600 ml/1 pt water until reduced by half.
Apply this liquid to the chilblain and add a dab of sesame oil to the affected area.

CHILDBIRTH, abdominal discomfort after:

Take 400 g/1 lb eggplant (aubergine), 50 g/2 oz raw brown sugar, 75 ml/3 fl oz brandy;
boil all together in 1·2 l/2 pt water until reduced by half.
Divide the results into 2 halves.
Eat each portion in the same day.

CHOLESTEROL, high:

There are several remedies for this, of which you should choose one.

1. Eat 125 g/5 oz oatmeal every day for breakfast.
2. Take 75 g/3 oz fresh black Chinese mushrooms (or 50 g/2 oz dried); cook and eat once daily.
3. Take 10 ripe hawthorn berries, 50 g/2 oz raw brown sugar;
   boil in 600 ml/1 pt water until reduced by half.
   Drink the results 2 or 3 times daily.
4. Take 25 g/1 oz raw onion before each meal (3 times daily).

COMMON COLD:

Prevention and relief:

75 g/3 oz spring onion boiled in 750 ml/1¼ pt water until reduced by half.
Drink while the liquid is hot and continue to do this once or twice a day for 3 to 4 days.

Relief:

12 g/½ oz fresh ginger, 25 g/1 oz brown sugar; boil in 250 g/12 fl oz water until reduced by half.
Drink while hot twice daily.

CONSTIPATION:

A problem which is obviously as common among the Chinese as among Europeans, judging by the variety of remedies. We suggest you start with a simple remedy and, if your problem remains stubborn, try others. It would be safe to combine more than one for this ailment.

1. Mix 2 teaspoonfuls rock salt with hot water.
   Drink result.
   Twice daily.
2. Eat 1 orange 3 times daily.
3. Blend 125 g/5 oz plums.
   Drink.
   Twice daily.
4. Drink 25 ml/1 fl oz fresh mulberry juice 2 or 3 times daily.
5. Mix 50 g/2 oz honey with 450 ml/¾ pt warm water.
   Drink half in the morning and half in the evening.
6. Eat 2 to 3 bananas early in the morning on an empty stomach.

7. Make a spinach soup, adding a small amount of salt.
   Drink this.
8. Take 25 g/1 oz crushed black sesame seed and mix with 150 ml/¼ pt hot water
   Drink the mixture.
9. Cook 300 g/12 oz lettuce in 75 g/3 oz peanut oil and small quantity of water.
   Eat.
10. Take 2 tablespoonfuls freshly juiced raw potato, 1 tablespoon honey, a little hot water; mix together and drink once a day before breakfast.
    Continue for 20 to 30 days.
11. Take 250 ml/10 fl oz cold milk, 75 g/3 oz mashed banana;
    mix them together and drink.
12. Eat one or two apples twice daily, morning and evening. Eat them on an empty stomach.

COUGH:

There are several remedies of which you should choose one. If there are no satisfactory results after a few days, change to another one.

1. Take 400 g/1 lb fresh mulberries, 50 g/2 oz honey;
   boil them together into a paste.
   Take 2 tablespoonfuls 2 to 3 times daily.
2. Juice 800 g/2 lb celery and 1 teaspoonful salt;
   boil them together in an earthenware pot.
   Drink 250 g/10 oz at dawn and in the evening.

3. Skin 400 g/1 lb of papaya, steam it and dip it in honey;
   cut into 100-g/4-oz chunks.
   Eat 4 times daily.
4. Take 2 bananas, 50 g/2 oz raw brown sugar;
   simmer in 250 ml/10 fl oz water until reduced to 150 ml/6 fl oz;
   Drink twice daily.
   Continue for 4 to 6 days.
5. Take 150 g/6 oz peanuts, 50 g/2 oz dried dates, 50 g/2 oz honey;
   boil in 1·2 l/2 pt water until reduced to half.
   Drink the liquid twice daily.
6. Take 25 g/1 oz French beans, 10 dried red dates;
   boil in 450 ml/¾ pt water until reduced to half.
   Eat and drink once daily.
   Continue for 4 to 7 days.
7. Take 12 g/½ oz apricot kernels and crush them;
   boil in 250 g/10 fl oz water until reduced by half.
   Drink once daily.

COUGH, chronic cough in children:

Take 250 g/10 oz saltwater eel, 50 g/2 oz black beans;
boil in 1·2 l/2 pt water until reduced by half.
Eat and drink in 2 portions per day.

COUGH, dry:

Take 100 g/4 oz black sesame seed and crush them,
add 50 g/2 oz raw brown sugar;
Eat 12 g/½ oz of this mixture morning and night.

COUGH, phlegm:

Take 25 g/1 oz black pepper, 250 g/10 oz fresh fish such as trout, 75 g/3 oz tomatoes;
boil them all together in 1·8 l/3 pt water until reduced to 600 ml/1 pt.
Drink lukewarm.

DEBILITY:

There are several remedies for this, all of them very nourishing. Choose one, since adding more might be too rich for the body suffering from physical weakness.

1. Take 600 ml/1 pt milk, 1·8 l/3 pt water;
   boil and reduce to 600 ml/1 pt.
   Drink 125 ml/5 fl oz 3 times daily.
   Continue for 2 to 3 months.
2. Take 200 g/8 oz pork, 100 g/4 oz brown rice;
   boil in 1·2 l/2 pt water until reduced to 400 ml/1½ pt.
   Drink and eat results.
3. Take 1 whole chicken and boil in 1·2 l/2 pt white wine (preferably rice wine) until reduced to 600 ml/1 pt.
   Eat and drink 2 or 3 times a week.
4. Take 200 g/8 oz pork and 100 g/4 oz brown rice;
   boil in 1·5 l/2½ pt water until reduced to 900 ml/1½ pt.
   Eat and drink results.
5. Take 400 g/1 lb perch, 25 g/1 oz spring onions, 6 g/¼ oz fresh ginger, some salt and some soy sauce;
   put flavourings on the fish, then steam.

Eat.
Do this 3 times a week.

DIABETES:

There are several remedies for this condition and, additionally, the Chinese traditionally used to eat the pancreas of the pig for the same purpose, as part of their general theory or organotherapy – eating the organ of the animal which corresponds to the weak organ of the human being. Although this has been dismissed as largely superstitious, many Chinese traditional healers feel that, since it is accepted as therapy for the liver and partially for the pancreas, it is time it was actually researched more by the sceptical before being dismissed out of hand.

1. Boil 150 g/6 oz fresh peas in a little water without salt.
   Eat them.
2. Juice 400 g/1 lb celery and boil the juice.
   Take 1 small cup 3 times daily for 2 to 3 weeks.
3. Take 150 g/6 oz snails, 100 g/4 oz rice wine; boil in 900 ml/1½ pt water until reduced to 450 ml/¾ pt.
   Eat and drink once daily.

DIARRHOEA:

The number of remedies for this indicates that it too was a common condition in China. We feel these will be most useful.

1. Take one clove of raw garlic and toast it in a dry pan until brown.

Eat it.
Do this 3 times daily.

2. Drink 200 ml/8 fl oz fresh guava juice twice daily.
3. Take 150 g/6 oz beef and boil in 600 ml/1 pt water until reduced to half;
divide into 2 and eat twice daily.
4. Take 25 g/1 oz dried powdered apples and mix with 125 g/5 oz warm water.
Drink before eating 3 times daily.
5. Toast 150 g/6 oz buckwheat;
when dry, grind into powder;
mix 12 g/½ oz with warm water and swallow.
Do this twice daily.
6. Take 50 g/2 oz toasted wheat, 50 g/2 oz toasted rice, 25 g/1 oz raw brown sugar;
mix them all together in hot water.
Eat the mixture.
7. Boil rice in water and drink the water.

DIARRHOEA, chronic:

Take 100 g/4 oz raw carrots, 50 g/2 oz raw brown sugar;
boil them in 900 ml/1½ pt water until reduced by half.
Eat and drink it all.

DRY MOUTH:

Take 150 g/6 oz sugar cane juice and 1 teaspoonful ginger juice;
mix and drink.

DYSENTERY, early stages:

Take 50 g/2 oz fresh hawthorn berries, 75 g/3 oz brown sugar;
boil in 600 ml/1 pt water until reduced to 300 ml/½ pt.
Drink while hot 2 or 3 times daily.

DYSENTERY:

Mash raw garlic into boiled water and drink the mixture.

ECZEMA:

Grate enough raw potato to make a covering for the eczema patch;
spread it on and put on a dressing of a clean bandage.
Change the dressing 4 to 6 times daily.
If the eczema is on the face, lie down for an hour or so while the poultice is on.

EYES, bloodshot:

Drink one big glass of tomato juice daily for breakfast or eat 2 or 3 raw tomatoes instead.

EYES, inflamed:

Take 150 g/6 oz snails, 100 g/4 oz pork, 12 g/½ oz fresh coriander;
boil in 1·2 l/2 pt water until reduced to 600 ml/1 pt.
Eat and drink once daily.

EYES, sore:

Put 1 teaspoonful rock salt into 1 cup hot water and mix the two together.
Drink.
Do this twice daily, morning and bedtime.

FATIGUE:

Take 250 g/10 oz lamb, 25 g/1 oz fresh ginger, 25 g/1 oz garlic;
boil in 1·8 l/3 pt water until reduced by half.
Eat and drink 125 g/5 oz twice daily.

HAEMORRHOIDS:

Eat 1 orange 3 times daily.

or

Eat 2 bananas early in the morning on an empty stomach.

or

Take 400 g/1 lb saltwater eel, 25 g/1 oz spring onions, some soy sauce, some peanut oil;
pour the flavourings over the eel and steam.
Eat.
Repeat this 2 or 3 times weekly.

HAIR loss:

Take one large piece of fresh ginger, peel it, dip into brandy and rub the scalp all over.
Do this twice daily.

HEPATITIS:

Eat 75–100 g/3–4 oz fresh white mushrooms 3 times daily.

or

Take 100 g/4 oz fresh grapes and boil in 600 ml/1 pt water until reduced by half.
Drink and eat the result once daily.

HICCOUGHS:

There are two remedies. Choose one.

1. Take 250 ml/10 fl oz milk, 25 ml/1 fl oz ginger juice, 25 g/1 oz raw brown sugar;
   boil for ten minutes.
   Drink while hot.
2. Take 25 ml/1 fl oz ginger juice and 25 g/1 oz honey;
   mix them and drink this.
   Repeat once or twice daily.

HYPERACIDITY:

Take 8 clams, toasted in their shells, and eat the clams.
Do this twice daily.

HYPERTENSION:

There are numerous remedies for hypertension. Choose one and stick with it for two or three months to give it a chance to work. Hypertension takes a long time to build up and therefore it needs an equally long time to subside.

1. Take a little vinegar (rice or cider) daily in your meals.
2. Drink one big glass of tomato juice each morning for breakfast or eat 2 or 3 raw tomatoes instead.
3. Take 400 g/1 lb celery and juice it;
   mix it with boiled water and drink while warm.
4. Take 75 g/3 oz raw crushed sunflower seeds, mix with 150 g/6 oz celery juice;
   drink.
   Do this twice daily.
   Continue for 20 to 30 days.

5. Take 50 g/2 oz fresh black Chinese mushrooms (or 75 g/3 oz dried);
   cook and eat them.
   Do this once a day.
6. Take 400 g/1 lb fresh apples and eat throughout the day in 3 helpings.
   Continue for 1 to 2 months.
7. Take 2 banana skins and boil them in 600 ml/1 pt water until reduced to half.
   Drink this liquid 3 or 4 times a day.
8. Take 10 fresh hawthorn berries, 50 g/2 oz raw brown sugar;
   boil in 600 ml/1 pt water until reduced by half.
   Drink the liquid 2 to 3 times daily.
9. Take 75 g/3 oz mussels, 200 g/8 oz celery;
   boil in 600 ml/1 pt water until reduced to 300 ml/½ pt.
   Repeat this 2 to 3 times a week.
10. Take 25 g/1 oz coriander, 75 g/3 oz freshwater fish, 25 g/1 oz garlic, 75 g/3 oz celery, 25 g/1 oz spring onions;
    boil together in 600 ml/1 pt water until reduced by half.
    Drink.
11. Take 1 large clove garlic, 1 onion, 100 g/4 oz celery, 200 g/8 oz carrot, 25 g/1 oz spring onions;
    boil together in 1·2 l/2 pt water until reduced by ⅔.
    Drink this.
    Repeat 2 or 3 times per week.
12. Take 150 g/6 oz raw peanut shells and boil them in 1·2 l/2 pt water until reduced by half.

Drink the liquid 3 times daily.
Do this for 3 or 4 weeks.
Do not add salt since this neutralizes the action of the peanut shells.

13. Take 150 g/6 oz of the silky threads attached to a corn cob and boil them in 900 ml/1½ pt water until reduced by half.
    Drink the liquid 4 or 5 times daily.
    Do not eat the threads.
14. Take 75 g/3 oz fresh broad beans (plus 50 g/2 oz broad bean flowers, if possible) and boil them in 600 ml/1 pt water until reduced by half.
    Drink the liquid 4 or 5 times a day.
15. Take 75 g/3 oz abalone, 25 g/1 oz abalone shell, 50 g/2 oz dried chrysanthemums;
    boil all together in 900 ml/1½ pt water until reduced to 450 ml/¾ pt.
    Eat and drink once daily.
    Repeat 2 to 4 times weekly.
16. Take 25 g/1 oz raw onion before each meal (3 times daily).

IMPOTENCE:

There are several remedies of which you should choose one and stick with it. Each of these remedies works on tonifying the kidneys, since deficient kidneys are considered to be the major cause of impotence.

1. Eat 75 g/3 oz fresh walnuts once a day for 30 to 40 days.
2. Steam 250 g/10 oz fresh shrimps and eat with brandy once a day for 10 to 20 days.

3. Take 100 g/4 oz mussels, 100 g/4 oz pork, 50 g/2 oz garlic, 100 g/4 oz potatoes;
   boil in 1·2 l/2 pt water until reduced to 600 ml/1 pt.
   Eat and drink once a day.
   Continue this for 6 to 12 days.
4. Take 1 pigeon and prepare it for cooking;
   bury it in 1·2–1·6 kg/3–4 lb crude rock salt;
   let it cook slowly in a crockpot for 2 to 3 hours.
   Eat it.
   Do this 3 to 4 times weekly.

INDIGESTION:

There are several suggested remedies for this and we advise you start with the easiest which are designed to get the digestive juices flowing and to avoid an individual instance of indigestion. If your condition is more long-term, try the more complex remedies which are intended to restore harmony to the digestive organs over a longer period of time.

1. Drink 150 ml/6 fl oz freshly blended pineapple juice once or twice daily.
2. Eat 150 g/6 oz papaya 3 times daily after meals.
3. Take 50 g/2 oz fresh coriander and blend it with a small amount of sesame oil.
   Eat it.
4. Take 25 g/1 oz chilli (fresh or powder), 100 ml/4 fl oz wine or cider vinegar, 12 g/½ fl oz soy sauce and mix them all together.
   Take 1 teaspoonful before and after each meal.

5. Take 150 g/6 oz cauliflower, 12 ml/½ fl oz garlic juice, 3 ml/⅛ fl oz ginger juice;
   mix together;
   divide into 3 portions.
   Eat 3 times a day.
6. Take 3 quails, pluck and gut them;
   bury in crude rock salt in a crockpot;
   slow-cook for several hours.
   Eat.
   Do this 2 or 3 times a week.

INDIGESTION, hyperacidity:
Take 50 g/2 oz guava powder and eat 12 g/½ oz 3 times daily with warm water half an hour after each meal.

INFLUENZA:
Eat 2 or 3 cloves of raw garlic 2 or 3 times daily.

INJURY:
Peel some taro root and put 150 g/6 oz in a blender;
add 150 g/6 oz fresh ginger and mix in 200 g/8 oz flour;
add water and make it into a paste.
Spread this paste on the wound.

INSOMNIA:
In Chinese medicine, insomnia has different causes according to the organ which is out of harmony. Therefore, you may like to try each of these for 2 or 3 days and note which one works for you.

1. Take 50 g/2 oz fresh walnuts, 50 g/2 oz black sesame seeds and crush and mix together;

make into 3-g/⅛-oz pills.
Eat 3 pills 3 times daily.

2. Take 75 g/3 oz wheat kernels, 15 dried dates and 25 g/1 oz honey;
   boil them together in 600 ml/1 pt water until reduced by half.
   Eat and drink the results of this.
3. Take 75 g/3 oz fresh oysters, 75 g/3 oz peanuts, 50 g/2 oz celery;
   boil in 1·2 l/2 pt water until reduced to 600 ml/1 pt.
   Eat and drink half and do this twice daily.
   Continue for 7 to 14 days.
4. Take 25 g/1 oz fresh mulberries and boil in 150 ml/6 fl oz water until reduced to half.
   Drink and eat 3 times daily.

INSOMNIA caused by anaemia:

Take 250 g/10 oz duck meat, 100 g/4 oz pork, 12 g/½ oz fresh ginger;
boil in 1·2 l/2 pt water until reduced by half.
Eat and drink the results.
Do this 2 or 3 times a week.

INSOMNIA caused by hypertension:

Take 100 g/4 oz celery and boil in 600 ml/1 pt water until reduced by half.
Drink before bedtime.

ITCHING:

Take 2 pigeons, 125 g/5 oz mung beans and boil in 1·2 l/2 pt water until reduced to 600 ml/1 pt.
Eat and drink.
Do this 2 or 3 times weekly.

JAUNDICE:

Take an old cucumber (with stem and root as well, if possible) and boil 200 g/8 oz in 750 ml/1¼ pt water until reduced by half.
Eat the cucumber and drink the liquid in 3 helpings throughout 1 day.
Continue as long as jaundice is present.

KIDNEY deficiency:

Take 250 g/10 oz fresh shrimps, steam them and eat with brandy once daily.
Continue this for 10 to 20 days.

LACTATION, congested:

1. Take 400 g/1 lb carp, 100 g/4 oz rice and boil in 1·8 l/3 pt water until reduced by half.
   Eat and drink half this amount twice daily.
2. Take 200 g/8 oz lightly fried shrimps and boil in 600 ml/1 pt rice wine.
   Eat and drink 150 g/6 oz twice a day.
   Continue for 3 to 4 days.

LACTATION, insufficient:

There are several remedies here, so choose one and stick with it.

1. Take 100 g/4 oz barley shoots and boil them in 600 ml/1 pt water until reduced by half.
   Drink the liquid but do not eat the shoots.
2. Take 400 g/1 lb papaya, 200 g/8 oz fish and boil in 1·8 l/3 pt water until reduced by half.
   Eat and drink the results.
3. Take 400 g/1 lb pig's knuckle, 100 g/4 oz peanuts

and boil in 1·8 l/3 pt water until reduced to 1·2 l/2 pt;
add some salt.
Eat and drink the results.

LARYNGITIS:

1. Take 125 g/5 oz dried figs, 50 g/2 oz molasses sugar and boil in 1·2 l/2 pt water until reduced by half.
   Eat and drink 125 g/5 oz a time, once or twice daily.

or

2. Take 100 g/4 oz peanuts, minus their brown skins, add a little salt and boil in 750 ml/1¼ pt water until reduced by half.
   Eat and drink.

LEGS, weakness in:

Take 125 g/5 oz minced beef, 2 slices fresh ginger and boil for 10 minutes in 450 ml/¾ pt water.
Eat and drink while hot at night-time.

LEUCORRHOEA:

Take 50 g/2 oz fresh beans, 50 g/2 oz raw brown sugar and cook with a little water.
Eat once daily.
Continue for 7 to 10 days.

LIVER SCLEROSIS: Eat 2 or 3 ripe plums daily.

LYMPH glands, swollen:

Take 800 g/2 lb eel (saltwater), toast until dry and then grind into powder.

Put 6 g/¼ oz into warm water and drink this dose twice daily.

LYMPH glands, swollen lymph glands in children:
Take 150 g/6 oz fresh oyster, 100 g/4 oz abalone and boil in 900 ml/1½ pt water until reduced to 450 ml/¾ pt.
Eat and drink the results.
Do this 3 or 4 times weekly.

MEASLES, in children:
Take 100 g/4 oz carrot, 12 g/½ oz parsley, 4 water chestnuts and boil all together in 1·2 l/2 pt water until reduced to half.
Drink once a day until well.
Note: If you cannot obtain fresh water chestnuts (usually available in Chinese supermarkets or speciality food stores), you can use tinned but then you must double the amount.

MENSTRUATION, irregular:
Take 75 g/3 oz raw brown sugar, 75 g/3 oz dried dates, 12 g/½ oz ginger and boil in 600 ml/1 pt of water until reduced to half.
Drink once daily.

or

Take one pigeon and pluck and clean;
bury in 1·2–1·6 kg/3–4 lb crude rock salt in a crock-pot;
cook for 2 to 3 hours.
Eat.
Do this 3 or 4 times weekly.

MENSTRUATION, late:

Take 400 g/1 lb squid, 100 g/4 oz black beans, 12 g/½ oz fresh ginger and some salt;
steam over 600 ml/1 pt water.
Eat half the amount twice daily.
Continue for 4 to 6 days.

MENSTRUATION, painful:

Take 12 g/½ oz fresh ginger, 25 g/1 oz raw brown sugar and boil in 600 ml/1 pt water until reduced by half.
Drink while hot once or twice daily.

MORNING SICKNESS: see Pregnancy, vomiting

NAUSEA:

Peel 1 orange, bruise the skin and smell it.

or

Take 250 ml/10 fl oz fresh whole milk, 25 ml/1 fl oz ginger juice, 25 g/1 oz raw brown sugar;
boil for 10 minutes.
Drink slowly while hot.

NERVOUS BREAKDOWN:

Anyone suffering from a nervous breakdown needs tonifying foods which will build up the body organs and strengthen the nervous system. Also study the list of stimulating foods and steadily include them, maintaining a balance with the calming foods as well.
Take 50 g/2 oz fresh walnuts, 50 g/2 oz black sesame seeds and crush them together;
make them into 3-g/⅛-oz pills.
Eat 3 pills 3 times a day.

NERVOUS TENSION:

Take 75 g/3 oz fresh oysters, 75 g/3 oz peanuts, 50 g/2 oz celery and boil in 1·2 l/2 pt water until reduced to 600 ml/1 pt.
Divide into 2 halves and eat and drink twice daily.
Continue for 7 to 14 days.

NIGHT BLINDNESS:

Night blindness is associated with liver deficiency, since the Chinese connect the liver with sight. Therefore, these remedies nourish the liver.

1. Drink 1 cup fresh carrot juice daily for 10 to 20 days.
2. Take 400 g/1 lb cod, 25 g/1 oz garlic, 6 g/¼ oz pepper, some salt;
   boil in 1·2 l/2 pt water until reduced by half.
   Eat and drink the results.
   Do this 2 or 3 times weekly.
3. Take 75 g/3 oz abalone, 1 abalone shell, 50 g/2 oz dried chrysanthemum flowers;
   boil in 900 ml/1½ pt water until reduced to 450 ml/¾ pt.
   Eat and drink once daily.
   Do this 2 to 4 times weekly.

NOSEBLEEDS:

Take 400 g/1 lb catfish, 25 g/1 oz spring onions, some salt;
steam and eat.
Do this 3 times a week.

or

Take a handful of dried broad-bean flowers and grind them into powder;

put 6 g/¼ oz in warm water 3 times daily.
Drink.

OEDEMA:

Take 400 g/1 lb raw peanuts and leave the brown skins on them;
add 150 g/6 oz raw brown sugar and boil in 1·2 l/2 pt water until reduced to 900 ml/1½ pt.
Drink this daily instead of water. You can also eat the peanuts, if you wish.
Do this for 7 days.

OEDEMA, due to weak heart:

Drink 125 ml/5 fl oz fresh coconut juice 2 or 3 times daily.

PAIN, abdominal:

Take 400 g/1 lb eggplant (aubergine), 50 g/2 oz raw brown sugar, 75 ml/3 fl oz brandy and boil them all in 1·2 l/2 pt water until reduced to half.
Eat and drink the results.

PAIN, stomach:

Take 2 tablespoonfuls freshly juiced potato, 1 tablespoonful honey and mix them in a little water.
Drink once a day before breakfast.
Continue this for 20 to 30 days.

PARASITES, roundworms and pinworms:

Eat 50–75 g/2–3 oz raw sunflower seeds daily for 7 to 10 days.

PHARYNGITIS:

Blend 3 pears, add 50 g/2 oz honey and mix with 600 ml/1 pt water;
boil and reduce to half.
Drink twice daily, half each time.

PHLEGM:

Take 1 pear, 7 spring onions (with roots, if possible), 75 g/3 oz raw brown sugar;
boil in 600 ml/1 pt water until reduced by half.
Eat and drink twice daily, using half each time.

POISONING, shellfish:

Make 125 ml/5 fl oz fresh olive juice.
Drink twice daily.

PREGNANCY, oedema:

Take 400 g/1 lb carp, 100 g/4 oz brown rice and boil in 1·8 l/3 pt water until reduced by half.
Eat and drink half twice daily.

PREGNANCY, vomiting:

Take 12 g/½ oz fresh ginger, 12 g/½ oz dried orange peel and boil in 600 ml/1 pt water until reduced by half.
Drink while hot.

PROSTATE gland, infected:

Eat 75 g/3 oz raw sunflower seeds 2 or 3 times daily.

RESTLESSNESS:

Eat boiled rice.

RHEUMATISM:

Take 100 g/4 oz fresh grapes and boil in 600 ml/1 pt water until reduced by half.
Eat and drink.

RHEUMATISM pain:

Take 400 g/1 lb eel, 75 g/3 oz pork and boil in 1·2 l/2 pt water until reduced by half.
Eat and drink.
Do this 2 or 3 times weekly.

or

Take 400 g/1 lb chicken on the bone, 75 g/3 oz garlic and boil in 1·2 l/2 pt water until reduced to 600 ml/1 pt.
Split into 3 portions.
Eat 125 g/5 oz 3 times daily.

ROUNDWORMS:

Take 800 g/1 lb saltwater eel, 600 ml/1 pt rice wine and some salt; boil until reduced by half.
Eat 200–250 g/8–10 oz with a little vinegar (cider or rice).
Do this 3 times weekly.

STOMACH, deficient:

Take 25 g/1 oz pepper, 100 g/4 oz beef and boil in 600 ml/1 pt water until reduced by half.
Eat and drink the result.

or

Take 150 g/6 oz goose meat, 50 g/2 oz garlic, 6 g/¼ oz fresh ginger;
boil in 600 ml/1 pt water until reduced to half.
Eat and drink the results.
Do this 2 or 3 times a week.

STOMACH pain:

Take 50 g/2 oz guava fruit powder and put 12 g/½ oz into warm water.
Drink this and repeat the dose 3 times daily after meals.

STOMACH, weak:

Eat 150 g/6 oz yoghurt (must be live with no artificial additives) for breakfast every day.

STONE, bladder:

Take 150 g/6 oz of the silken threads attached to a corn cob and boil in 900 ml/1½ pt water until reduced to half.
Drink the liquid 4 or 5 times a day. Do not eat the threads.

STOOL, bloody:

Take 100 g/4 oz beancurd, 50 g/2 oz raw brown sugar and boil together in a small quantity of water. Eat.

SUNSTROKE:

There are several remedies for this. The first removes heat from the body and the rest reduce heat and replace lost liquid. Continue the treatment until symptoms have subsided.

1. Juice some garlic and apply a few drops of the juice just inside the nostrils.
   This will hurt, but it is very effective in counteracting the heatstroke aspects of sunstroke.
2. Juice 75 g/3 oz French beans and mix with a small amount of warm water.
   Drink this mixture twice daily.

3. Blend 125 g/5 oz fresh pineapple and drink.
   Do this twice daily.
4. Juice 150 g/6 oz fresh watermelon and drink.
   Do this twice daily.
5. Boil 100 g/4 oz mung beans in 600 ml/1 pt water until reduced by half.
   Eat and drink the results.

SWEATING, cold:
Take 600 ml/1 lb buckwheat flour, 100 g/4 oz raw brown sugar, add water;
bake until ready. Makes approximately 12 biscuits.
Eat 3 or 4 of these biscuits daily.

SWEATING, excess:
Take 75 g/3 oz fresh oyster, 25 g/1 oz oyster shells and boil in 900 ml/1½ pt water until reduced to 300 ml/½ pt.
Eat and drink twice daily.

SWELLING:
Take 150 g/6 oz beef and boil in 600 ml/1 pt water until reduced to half.
Divide into 2 and eat twice daily.

TAPEWORM:
Take one fresh coconut, drink the juice and eat 100 g/4 oz of the flesh in the morning on an empty stomach. Then do not eat for 4 hours.
Do this daily.

THIRST:
Eat raw cucumber or juice one and drink it.

THROAT, fishbone in the throat:

Take 200 ml/8 fl oz warm boiled vinegar (wine, cider or rice).
Sip slowly, pausing frequently.
After finishing this, chew a large piece of bread and swallow it in one big gulp.

THROAT, sore throat:

1. Mix 1 teaspoonful rock salt into 1 cup hot water.
   Drink the liquid.
   Do this twice a day in the morning and the evening.
2. Take 50 g/2 oz dried tangerine skin and boil in 600 ml/1 pt water until reduced by half.
   Store in a vacuum flask and drink throughout the day as tea.
3. Take 12 olives, 25 g/1 oz spring onions and boil in 600 ml/1 pt water until reduced by half.
   Drink and eat the result in 2 portions.
4. Take 400 g/1 lb watercress, 200 g/8 oz pig's knuckle and boil in 2·4 l/4 pt water until reduced by half.
   Drink and eat.

THROAT, sore and dry:

Take 100 g/4 oz watermelon skin and boil in 600 ml/1 pt water until reduced by half.
Drink 2 or 3 times daily.

TIGHT CHEST:

Eat spinach soup.

TINNITUS:

Take 75 g/3 oz mussels, 200 g/8 oz celery and boil in 600 ml/1 pt water until reduced by half.
Eat and drink.
Do this 2 or 3 times weekly.

or

Take 1 400 g/1 lb catfish, 100 g/4 oz mung beans, 6 g/¼ oz garlic;
boil in 1·8 l/3 pt water until reduced by half.
Drink 250 g/10 oz twice a day.
Do this 3 times weekly.

TOOTHACHE:

Add 1 teaspoonful rock salt to 1 cup hot water and mix together.
Drink.
Do this twice daily, in the morning and at bedtime.

ULCER, mouth:

Eat 400 g/1 lb watermelon in 2 sections per day.
Apply a dab of raw brown sugar powder to the ulcer after eating the watermelon.

ULCER, stomach (early stages):

Juice 200 g/8 oz cabbage and warm it up.
Drink twice daily before eating.
Continue for 10 to 20 days.

URINATION, frequent:

Take 50 g/2 oz fresh walnuts, toast them until brown;
warm a glass of rice wine.
Eat and drink the two together.
Do this once or twice daily.

URINATION, painful:

Take 75 g/3 oz sweet corn and boil in 600 ml/1 pt water until reduced by half.
Drink the liquid and do not eat the sweet corn.
Repeat this remedy 2 or 3 times a day, making a fresh lot each time.

URINATION, retention of urine:

There are a number of remedies for this, out of which you should choose one.

1. Eat carrots.
2. Take a dried eggplant (aubergine) and grind it into powder.
   Take 12 g/½ oz of this powder in warm water, 3 times daily.
   To dry the eggplant, put it on a metal tray and grill or roast it gently until dry.
3. Juice 100 g/4 oz mung bean sprouts, add 25 g/1 oz raw brown sugar and mix with 150 ml/¼ pt boiling water.
   Drink while warm.
4. Eat 200–300 g/8–12 oz raw lettuce once daily.
5. Eat spinach soup.

URINATION, sluggish:

There are several remedies for this, the first four of which stimulate the bladder into production of urine and the last two of which tonify the kidneys and bladder.

1. Drink 100–125 ml/4–5 fl oz fresh plum juice daily.
2. Drink 125 ml/5 fl oz fresh tangerine juice daily or eat 3 to 4 tangerines.

3. Drink 150 ml/6 fl oz pear juice for breakfast daily.
4. Juice 75 g/3 oz fresh peas and drink the liquid. Do this twice daily.
5. Cook and eat boiled rice.
6. Take 125 g/5 oz clams, 50 g/2 oz garlic, 50 g/2 oz spring onions;
   boil all together in 900 ml/1½ pt water until reduced to 600 ml/1 pt.
   Eat and drink once daily.

VOICE, loss of:

Take 125 g/5 oz dried figs, 50 g/2 oz raw brown sugar and boil in 1·2 l/2 pt water until reduced to 600 ml/1 pt.
Divide into 2 halves and eat and drink both in 1 day.

or

Blend 3 pears and 50 g/2 oz honey, mixed in 600 ml/1 pt water;
boil until reduced by half.
Divide into 2 halves and eat and drink both in 1 day.

VOMITING:

Blend 50 g/2 oz fresh ginger in 100 ml/4 fl oz water;
warm up and drink.
Take 75 ml/3 fl oz each time twice daily.

WEIGHT, counteracting loss of weight:

Take 200 g/8 oz pork, 100 g/4 oz brown rice and boil in 1·5 l/2½ pt water until reduced to 900 ml/1½ pt.
Eat and drink.

Part Six

So You'd Rather be Yang? (or even Yin!)

There may be any number of reasons why a person decides to change or modify his own basic nature. It could be a philosophical decision, to develop into a more yin, inward-looking type. It could be a defensive measure against unwanted behaviour patterns, a way of controlling an over-aggressive fiery nature. It may be to explore the kind of life which seems more desirable, the withdrawn yin wishing to develop a more outgoing bold pattern of life and needing extra energy to draw upon to do this.

We are not really concerned with your reasons for wanting to become more yin or more yang, we would just like to urge that you bring the same essential to this as to everything else – harmonious balance. Therefore, by all means change your diet to a yin-producing or a yang-promoting one, but do it with moderation. We suggest that you try the fourteen-day yin or the fourteen-day yang diet and then, if you still wish to cultivate this new side to your nature, incorporate the necessary foods with their balancing side too. So, even if you wish to be more yin, be sure you do not make the mistake of eating nothing but yin foods. If you do this, you will actually become deficient and the organs of your body may begin to under-function. This will only lead to great disharmony which will mean that you will not benefit from being yin. You will merely become unhealthy.

We have put together two diets which will work to bring out your yin nature or your yang nature. If you follow these, you will certainly see some changes for yourself, but if you want to change the actual items on the menu, you can replace them with other appropriate foods by checking out the food section and working out what will fit into your yin or yang diet. We have simply saved you some time, but substitution on our menu is permitted. Of course, if you replace yin foods with yang ones – or the other way round – naturally you will not get the results you might want.

In these diets, as elsewhere in this book, we are basically giving you the ingredients and the correct cooking method. For details of how to cook such dishes, if you do not already know, you will have to consult a cookery book since our interest is your diet, not your kitchen processes.

The Harmony Fourteen-day Yang Diet:

We are working along the three-meals-a-day pattern, but many people are actually better off with little-and-often meals. If that is you, go ahead and do it. There are a great many people in the world today trying to persuade their unhappy body systems to fit into a three-meal-a-day pattern when it does not basically suit them. Make sure, whichever is your choice, that you stick to a regular pattern of eating. This is more important than the number of meals you eat. You will have better digestion, better absorption and a more harmonious body if you eat regularly. Make sure that every meal, however small, is balanced and – if you are following our fourteen-day energy-change regime – ensure that your choice of food fits the yin or yang bill.

By the way, if you eat five small meals a day instead of three, you do not put on any more weight. In fact, you may even lose it, since your body will digest food more efficiently and get rid of unwanted nutrients. It is not lack of food which leads to weight loss, it is thorough absorption and disposal of what you eat in harmony with your body needs. If your body organs are in harmonious balance with each other, you are much less likely to be overweight. Being overweight is most often a question of some imbalance of the way in which the organs are functioning. Many of the people who spend all their lives struggling with diets are actually at the mercy of their own out-of-sync body systems. The very imbalance of many of the diets they follow only serves to make their problem worse by further impairing the functions of their organs.

Yang Yourself in Fourteen Days

For breakfast, you can choose from among the following:

> cornflakes, eggs, beef tea, chicken broth, yoghurt, bread, butter, peanut butter, walnut cake, hot chocolate or any other yang items you want for breakfast.
>
> You can eat as many items as you like, but remember that the Chinese stop when their stomachs are 75 per cent full.

Monday: *(choose 2 or 3 items)*

Lunch:	*Dinner:*
beef soup	chicken soup
fried trout	steamed carp
lamb chops	roast pigeon

Substitute with any other yang item, selected from the list of stimulating foods contained in the food chapter. When choosing vegetables, add only those vegetables which are neutral.

You can add the following items to any meal throughout the fourteen days, since these are all powerfully yang: chestnuts, peanuts, walnuts, black grapes, cherries, stout, red wine, port, brandy, coffee. The nuts, of course, should not be roasted or salted since this causes imbalance in the body.

Tuesday: *(choose 2 or 3 items)*

Lunch:
shrimp cream chowder
braised freshwater eel/braised cod
hamburger steak/roast rabbit

Dinner:
chestnut and quail soup
steamed trout
venison stew/roast lamb
black date pie/cherry pie/grapes

Wednesday: *(choose 2 or 3 items)*

Lunch:
peanut and chicken soup
braised carp
venison stew/roast chicken/roast quail
lamb chop

Dinner:
venison soup/onion soup
fried shrimps
roast lamb/fried chicken
walnut cake

Thursday:

Lunch:
trout cream chowder
fried carp/fried trout/fried cod
roast veal

Dinner:
egg and sweet corn soup
barbecued eel
roast chicken
cherry pie/black grapes/cheese

Friday:

Lunch:
walnut and pigeon soup
steamed shrimps with chilli
venison steak/roast rabbit/fried chicken

Dinner:
garlic and eel soup/chicken soup with barley
fried trout/garlic squid
beef steak
peanut biscuits

Saturday:

Lunch:
lamb soup/chestnut soup/celery soup
steamed freshwater eel
braised beef/roast goose

Dinner:
carp soup
barbecued shrimp
curried chicken
grapes/pineapple/coconut pudding

Sunday:

Lunch:
brown rice and trout soup/celery soup
sautéed eel/fried chicken/chillied clams
roast pigeon

Dinner:
eat anything you want to, even a yin item

For the next seven days, we suggest you continue to juggle these high-yang items, remembering that at any point you can substitute with other stimulating foods if you wish to do so. Although some of the items are not necessarily standard table fare, we list these as some of the most powerful foods for producing yang reactions in the body system. Since you will be able to use the scarcer items for several dishes – as soup, as stew, as a starter or a main dish – we feel that it is well worth your while persisting with them.

We assume that you will add vegetables to every meal, according to availability and subject only to them being neutral or yang.

Yin Yourself in Fourteen Days

For breakfast, you may choose any of the following items:

oatmeal, eggs, ham, grapes or grape juice, bread, butter, honey.

You may drink milk, tea, coffee and you may eat any fruit from the following:

grapes, pears, mulberries, papaya.

Throughout the entire fourteen days, you may also have a little beer or white wine with any meal.

Monday:

Lunch:
clam chowder with cream/mushroom soup*
pork and carrots/rabbit stew
cod and spinach

Dinner:
codfish chowder with cream/watercress soup
steamed abalone/steamed oysters
roast duck/stuffed eggplant
cheese/banana pudding/pumpkin pie

*Not tinned mushroom soup, which is yang due to high sugar and salt content.

Tuesday:

Lunch:
pork and mung bean soup/kelp soup
egg and ham omelette
rabbit stew

Dinner:
clam soup/oyster soup/spinach soup
fried cod/frog's legs
steamed goose/baked snails
pear or mulberry pie

Wednesday:

Lunch:
mussel and spinach soup with cream
fried cod/fried oysters
sautéed duck with vegetables

Dinner:
catfish and black bean soup/tomato soup*
baked cod and cheese
sautéed liver and onions
roast pork
cheese or pears or papaya or grapes

Thursday:

Lunch:
codfish chowder with cream/watercress soup
eggs, mussels, raisins and fried rice
braised duck/egg and spinach with cheese sauce

Dinner:
duck soup/watercress soup/bean soup
braised catfish
roast rabbit
permitted fruit or cheese

*Not tinned, due to high salt and sugar content.

Friday:

Lunch:
spinach, egg and duck soup/potato soup
baked clams
roast goose

Dinner:
pork and carrot soup/watercress or tomato soup
steamed cod
sliced duck in coconut juice
baked rice
coconut milk pudding/fresh figs

Saturday:

Lunch:
mushroom soup
roast rabbit glazed with honey
fried codfish fingers

Dinner:
cauliflower soup
baked snails
baked rabbit with ginger and honey
banana pudding

Sunday:

Lunch:
pea soup
rabbit stew
frog's legs with garlic

Dinner:
eat anything you would like

As with the yang diet, you are recommended to substitute any items for those in the list of calming foods. We have tried to suggest something which will be interesting enough to test you as a cook, assuming you enjoy that, but if you do not, look at the list and make your own choice of items.

Most of these items are reasonably accessible in

cities. To get black beans, you might need to check with your nearest ethnic store – Chinese or West Indian or Indian. We really do not suggest that you use the quick-cooking rice available in packets but get the regular type.

Tonic Recipes

All the recipes contained in this section are intended to be applied, not so much for specific conditions, as for the regulating of specific organs. They are separated into stimulating, calming and neutral groups and, since they are not strictly medicinal in the precise way that the remedies in the common ailments chapter are, the reader may add whatever else he wishes to do in the way of enhancing the dish. It will be better to make the selection of additional ingredients from the same group of foods: if you want to make a stimulating dish, choose extra items from the list of stimulating foods in the food chapter. You may add any condiments you wish to and you may vary the way in which you cook the dish.

Since this is not a cookery book, as we have said before, in this section we only include the vital items for each recipe. To make the dishes more palatable, you must treat them in some way acceptable to yourself. While the point of the specific ailments remedies is to extract the medical qualities of the food – even if it does not taste very agreeable – the aim of this section is that you should make each of these suggestions as tasty as possible. So, feel free to add whatever else you wish to these very basic recipes.

If you are not sure which of the recipes would be best to make for yourself, consult the table which lists the common syndromes of the major organs.

As with the other remedies, you cannot do any harm to yourself by using any of these recipes since they are based upon ordinary everyday foods which you probably already use, but without being aware of the way in which they affect your body. You can use these recipes as a back-up to any formal medical treatment you are already receiving or you can devise an eating regime for yourself which you feel suits your needs.

To make things easier for you, we have linked each of these recipes with the particular body organ they affect and, to check this out, you should consult the section which immediately precedes this one. Since the recipes are all well balanced, you could make a diet sheet for yourself from your preferred dishes and follow it for as long as you wish to do so. The only thing you must always keep in mind is that harmony is the ultimate aim of every diet, since without harmony in the body, you cannot expect to find harmony in the mind or the spirit.

Table 9 *Common Syndromes of the Major Organs*

Heart:

Symptoms	*Tongue*	*Pulse*
Deficient		
quiet in mien, palpitations, shortness of breath, fatigue, cold sweat, tight chest, poor memory, facial oedema, numbness in the extremities	dilated pale tongue with thin white coating	small, weak, missed beat
Excess		
insomnia, irritability, chest pain, palpitations, fever	red, dry	large, strong, fast, irregular

Heart cont.		
delirium, stroke, neurosis, thirst, bitter taste in the mouth, pain in the tongue		

Small intestine:

Symptoms	*Tongue*	*Pulse*
Deficient		
abdominal pain, cold sweat, cold feeling in the abdomen, diarrhoea, indigestion	pale, feels tender, thin white coating	small, weak, slow
Excess		
restlessness, blood in urine, sluggish urination, pain in the penis, distension of abdomen, flatulence	red, dry, yellow coating	smooth, fast

Liver:

Symptoms	*Tongue*	*Pulse*
Deficient		
poor vision, dizziness, numbness in muscles and tendons, pain in scrotum, hernia pain, nervous insomnia, palpitations	blueish, white coating, wet	deep, tight, slow, weak
Excess		
red painful eyes, restlessness, irritability, thirst, bitter taste in the mouth, dark yellow urine, dizziness, migraine, pain in the ribs, numbness in fingers, ringing in the ears, tremors, cramps, restless in sleep	red, dry, yellow coating, tremor	tight, fast strong

Gall bladder:

Symptoms	*Tongue*	*Pulse*
Deficient		
dizziness, timidity, poor vision, chest discomfort, nausea, restlessness, insomnia	pale, thin white coating	tight, small, slow, weak
Excess		
irritability, anger, distension of chest, pain in ribs, nausea, vomiting, bitter taste in the mouth, hot and cold chills, vertigo, ringing in ears, sleeps a lot	red, yellow coating	tight, fast, strong

Lungs:

Symptoms	*Tongue*	*Pulse*
Deficient		
shortness of breath, cold sweat, cough, white watery sputum, cold feeling in chest and back, pale face, fatigue, numbness in hands, low voice	dilated, pale, thin white coating	small, weak, slow, sluggish
Excess		
thirst, sore throat, hoarse voice, asthma, dry nostrils, thick yellow sputum, constipation, tight chest, sluggish urination, fever, headaches	red, dry, yellow coating	strong, fast, rough

Large intestines:

Symptoms	*Tongue*	*Pulse*
Deficient		
abdominal pain, diarrhoea, prolapse of the anus, cold hands and feet, clear urine	pale, smooth white clear coating	deep, slow, weak, sluggish
Excess		
abdominal pain, constipation, hard stools, distension of abdomen, hiccoughs, burning pain in the anus, yellow urine with restricted flow, bad breath, dizziness, headaches	red, dry, yellow coating	fast, smooth, strong

Kidneys:

Symptoms	*Tongue*	*Pulse*
Deficient		
dizziness, blurred vision, ringing in the ears, poor hearing, lower-back pain, weakness in the legs, nocturnal emissions, premature ejaculation, impotence, cold feet, oedema in the feet, dry cough, pains in the joints	pale, dilated, white coating	weak
Excess		
powerful sexual drive, frequent erections, restless sleep, thirsty at night, yellow urine with restricted flow, hot flushes	red, dry, no coating	strong, fast

Bladder:

Symptoms	*Tongue*	*Pulse*
Deficient		
frequent urination, clear urine, oedema, dark complexion, enuresis	pale, dilated, with thin white coating	deep, small, tight, weak
Excess		
urine retention, dark yellow urine, pain in the penis, blood in the urine, abdominal distension	red, with yellow coating	deep, fast, tight, strong

Spleen:

Symptoms	*Tongue*	*Pulse*
Deficient		
poor appetite, indigestion, distension of abdomen, diarrhoea, loose stools, fatigue, thin, oedema, cold extremities, blood in the stools	pale, looks tender, thin white coating, wet	weak, slow, sluggish
Excess		
dry red lips, dry mouth, aching gums, mouth ulcers, bad breath, distension of stomach, thirst, hunger	red, dry, yellow coating	strong, fast

Stomach:

Symptoms	*Tongue*	*Pulse*
Deficient		
distension of stomach, belching, poor appetite, indigestion, stomach ache,	pale, white coating, wet	weak, deep, sluggish

Stomach cont.

Symptoms	*Tongue*	*Pulse*
vomiting, cold extremities, soft or liquid stool		
Excess		
thirst, good appetite, aching or bleeding gums, bad breath, stomach ache, distension of stomach, constipation	red, thick, yellow coating	smooth, fast, strong

Which tonic recipe do you need?

At the end of this chapter is a list of tonic recipes, each affecting one or more of the major organs. Here we tell you which recipe to refer to for a deficient or excess condition in any of your organs. First look through the checklist of common syndromes and see if any of them fit you. To do this thoroughly, you may well have to also look back at the other checklists in this book – the yin-yang table, the meridian table – since many individual symptoms appear in various states of excess or deficiency. You are looking for a whole picture of your health when deciding on the tonic recipes which can best help you.

Stimulating recipes for deficient conditions

Liver: see recipes 3, 14, 15, 16, 20, 31, 32, 33, 34, 35, 36, 37

Spleen: see recipes 6, 7, 8, 9, 12, 13, 17, 18, 19, 21, 22, 23, 24, 25, 26, 31, 32, 35, 36, 37

Stomach: see recipes 4, 5, 12, 13, 17, 18, 23, 24, 25, 26, 27, 28, 29, 30, 31, 32, 35, 37
Lungs: see recipes 6, 7, 8, 9, 10, 11, 14, 15, 16, 23, 24, 27, 28, 29, 30, 33, 34, 36, 37
Large intestine: see recipe 35
Kidneys: see recipes 1, 2, 3, 4, 5, 10, 11, 19, 20, 21, 22, 25, 26, 27, 28, 29, 30, 33, 34, 36

Calming recipes for excess conditions

Heart: see recipes 69, 70
Small intestine: see recipes 42, 43, 55, 56, 60, 61, 71, 72
Liver: see recipes 46, 47, 52, 53, 54, 57, 58, 59, 67, 68
Spleen: see recipes 38, 65, 66, 67, 68, 69, 70
Stomach: see recipes 39, 40, 41, 42, 43, 46, 47, 54, 55, 56, 57, 58, 59, 60, 61, 67, 68, 69, 70, 71, 72
Lungs: see recipes 44, 45, 48, 49, 50, 51, 62, 63, 64, 65
Large intestine: see recipes 39, 40, 41, 42, 43, 48, 49, 50, 51, 55, 56, 62, 63, 64, 65, 70, 71, 72
Kidneys: see recipes 44, 45, 52, 53, 66

Neutralizing recipes for the body organs

By the term neutral, we do not mean that they do nothing at all to the body. They nourish the organs with which they are related, but do not in any way change their balance.

Liver: see recipes 75, 76, 78, 88, 91
Spleen: see recipes 77, 79, 80, 81, 82, 83, 84, 85, 86, 87, 88, 89, 90, 91, 92
Stomach: see recipes 73, 74, 77, 79, 80, 91
Lungs: see recipes 78, 81, 82, 87, 88, 89, 90, 92
Large Intestine: see recipes 87, 92
Kidneys: see recipes 83, 84, 85, 86, 89, 90, 91, 92

Stimulating recipes

1. *Braised venison with vegetables*
   Affects: kidneys
   Take 250 g/10 oz venison, 100 g/4 oz carrots, 75 g/3 oz onion, 25 g/1 oz garlic, some soy sauce;
   add any other desired ingredients from the list of stimulating foods and braise until tender.

2. *Venison soup*
   Affects: kidneys
   Take 200 g/8 oz venison, 75 g/3 oz onion, 6 g/¼ oz fresh black pepper;
   add other neutral or stimulating items if you wish;
   boil in 1·8 l/3 pt water until reduced to half.

3. *Steamed cuttlefish (squid)*
   Affects: liver, kidneys
   Take 400 g/1 lb cuttlefish or squid, 6 g/¼ oz fresh ginger, some sugar, soy sauce, small amount of water;
   steam all together until fish is tender.

4. *Mixed corn soup*
   Affects: stomach, kidneys
   Take 100 g/4 oz sweet corn, 50 g/2 oz raw sliced chicken meat, 1 onion, 50 g/2 oz fresh cream;
   add selected condiments;
   boil the ingredients in water to taste.

5. *Sweet corn mixture*
   Affects: stomach, kidneys
   Take 75 g/3 oz sweet corn, 50 g/2 oz raw sliced pork, 25 g/1 oz green chilli, 50 g/2 oz fried peanuts;
   add condiments;
   stir-fry in vegetable oil.

6. *Braised peanuts and chilli*
   Affects: lungs, spleen
   Take 400 g/1 lb shelled peanuts with skins on, 200 g/8 oz chopped raw chicken, 25 g/1 oz garlic;
   add condiments to taste;
   stir-fry in vegetable oil.

7. *Stewed peanuts and pork*
   Affects: lungs, spleen
   Take 400 g/1 lb shelled peanuts with skins on, 200 g/8 oz sliced raw pork, 25 g/1 oz garlic;
   add condiments to taste;
   stew in small quantity of water.

8. *Peanut porridge*
   Affects: lungs, spleen
   400 g/1 lb roasted peanuts ground into powder;
   add water and raw brown sugar;
   boil and stir until it thickens.

9. *Peanut soup*
   Affects: lungs, spleen
   250 g/10 oz shelled peanuts, 125 g/5 oz sliced raw pork;

add condiments as necessary;
boil in 1·8 l/3 pt water until reduced by half.

10. *Roast pork*
Affects: lungs, kidneys
Take the desired quantity of shoulder of pork and coat with soy sauce mixed with sugar;
roast until done.

11. *Pigeon soup*
Affects: lungs, kidneys
Take 2 pigeons, add fresh black pepper, 6 g/¼ oz fresh ginger, 8 g/⅓ oz garlic and other desired ingredients;
boil all together in 900 ml/1½ pt water until reduced to 600 ml.

12. *Braised goose and vegetables*
Affects: stomach, spleen
Take 250 g/10 oz goose meat, 50 g/2 oz spring onions, 25 g/1 oz fresh ginger, some raw brown sugar, soy sauce and water;
braise until done.

13. *Steamed goose*
Affects: stomach, spleen
1 goose (gutted and cleaned), coat with soy sauce mixed with salt, then brush on olive oil;
put on grid in large pan and add water;
steam until done.

14. *Steamed fresh shrimps*
Affects: liver, lungs
Take 400 g/1 lb shrimps in shells, 25 g/2 oz

fresh ginger, 50 g/2 oz spring onions, some water;
suspend shrimps over water;
steam until done.

15. *Sautéed shrimp balls*
Affects: liver, lungs
Take 250 g/10 oz large shrimps (shelled), 50 g/2 oz garlic, 50 g/2 oz red chilli, a little salt and soy sauce;
chop everything small and form into balls;
sauté in a little water.

16. *Curried shrimps*
Affects: liver, lungs
Take 250 g/10 oz large shrimps (shelled), 100 g/4 oz curry sauce, 100 ml/4 fl oz coconut juice, 150 ml/¼ pt fresh milk, 25 ml/1 fl oz coconut oil;
add salt and other condiments;
simmer all together until done.

17. *Stewed beef and vegetables*
Affects: stomach, spleen (mild)
400 g/1 lb sliced raw beef, 75 g/3 oz tomatoes, 75 g/3 oz onion, 25 g/1 oz fresh ginger, some raw brown sugar, salt, soy sauce;
add water if necessary and simmer gently until done.

18. *Beef tea*
Affects: stomach, spleen
400 g/1 lb beef, 25 g/1 oz fresh ginger, other condiments as desired;
boil in 600 ml/1 pt water until reduced to half.

19. *Sautéed saltwater eel*
    Affects: spleen, kidneys
    Take 250 g/10 oz eel and chop it small, add 50 g/2 oz crushed garlic, some raw brown sugar, soy sauce, salt, peanut oil;
    sauté until done.

20. *Steamed mussels*
    Affects: liver, kidneys
    Take 800 g/2 lb mussels in their shells, 50 g/2 oz chopped garlic, 50 g/2 oz spring onions, some salt and other condiments;
    suspend over small quantity of water and steam.

21. *Garlic chicken*
    Affects: spleen, kidneys
    Take 800 g/2 lb chicken meat, chopped into bite-sized pieces, 150 g/6 oz garlic and add other condiments and stimulating or neutral vegetables as desired, peanut oil and a small quantity of water;
    braise gently until done.

22. *Garlic beef*
    Affects: spleen, kidneys
    Take 400 g/1 lb sliced beef, 100 g/4 oz garlic and other condiments to taste;
    put in small amount of peanut oil and small quantity of water;
    sauté until done.

23. *Stewed beef and carrots*
    Affects: spleen, stomach, lungs

Take 400 g/1 lb beef, 200 g/8 oz carrots, 1 onion;
chop onion and carrots and slice beef small;
add water, stock and condiments;
cook until ready.

24. *Carrot soup*

Affects: spleen, stomach, lungs
Take 100 g/4 oz carrots, 2 onions, 75 g/3 oz celery, 2 tomatoes, 100 g/4 oz sliced beef;
chop vegetables into small pieces;
boil all in water or stock to taste, adding necessary condiments.

25. *Sautéed lamb and mushrooms*

Affects: spleen, stomach, kidneys
200 g/8 oz lamb sliced small, 100 g/4 oz button or Chinese mushrooms, 25 g/1 oz spring onions;
add soy sauce and other necessary condiments;
sauté gently until done.

26. *Stewed lamb and black beans*

Affects: spleen, stomach, kidneys
400 g/1 lb lamb sliced small, 100 g/4 oz black beans, 12 g/½ oz fresh ginger, 12 g/½ oz spring onions, soy sauce, condiments, some water;
stew until done.

27. *Chicken and celery*

Affects: lungs, stomach, kidneys
Take 150 g/6 oz celery, 100 g/4 oz sliced

chicken meat, 100 g/4 oz carrots, add condiments and stock to taste;
boil until done.

28. *Ginger beef and celery*
Affects: lungs, stomach, kidneys
200 g/8 oz celery, 75 g/3 oz fresh ginger, 100 g/4 oz beef slices;
add soy sauce and condiments;
sauté in peanut oil and small quantity of water or stock.

29. *Frog's legs with celery*
Affects: lungs, stomach, kidneys
200 g/8 oz frog's legs, 150 g/6 oz ginger, 150 g/6 oz celery;
add condiments to taste;
sauté in peanut oil and small amount of water.

30. *Celery soup*
Affects: lungs, stomach, kidneys
125 g/5 oz celery, 2 onions, 100 g/4 oz carrots, 125 g/5 oz sliced beef;
chop and slice vegetables;
simmer in water or stock to taste.

31. *Braised chicken and chestnuts*
Affects: liver, spleen, stomach
400 g/1 lb sliced chicken, 150 g/6 oz peeled chestnuts, some soy sauce, raw brown sugar, ginger, sesame oil;
sauté in small quantity of peanut oil and water if desired.

32. *Chicken and pork soup*

Affects: liver, spleen, stomach
250 g/10 oz chopped chicken, 100 g/4 oz sliced pork, add stimulating or neutral vegetables as desired, add condiments;
boil in 1·5 l/2½ pt water until reduced to 900 ml/1½ pt.

33. *Chicken and walnuts*

Affects: lungs, kidneys, liver
Take 200 g/8 oz chopped chicken, 125 g/5 oz fresh walnuts, plus desired condiments;
sauté in small amount of peanut oil and water if necessary.

34. *Walnut porridge*

Affects: lungs, kidneys, liver
400 g/1 lb walnuts ground into powder, 100 g/4 oz raw brown sugar, add water;
boil gently until the mixture thickens, stirring continually;
eat chilled or warm.

35. *Chillied beef*

Affects: spleen, stomach, liver and large intestine
50 g/2 oz fresh chillis, 100 g/4 oz sliced beef, 1 onion, condiments to taste;
sauté in vegetable oil, plus stock or water if necessary.

36. *Braised carp*

Affects: spleen, lungs, liver, kidneys
400 g/1 lb carp, 50 g/2 oz ginger, 50 g/2 oz

spring onions, 25 g/1 oz garlic, some salt, raw brown sugar, soy sauce;
braise in vegetable oil.

37. *Sautéed cod and vegetables*
Affects: spleen, stomach, liver, lungs
400 g/1 lb cod, 100 g/4 oz carrots, 75 g/3 oz spring onions, 75 g/3 oz celery, some fresh black pepper, soy sauce;
sauté in peanut oil.

Calming recipes

38. *Rabbit stew*
Affects: spleen
200 g/8 oz rabbit, 100 g/4 oz carrot, 75 g/3 oz onion, 12 g/½ oz garlic, salt, soy sauce;
chop up the rabbit, slice the carrots and other vegetables;
add any other calming or neutral vegetables desired;
cook in stock or water, with condiments to taste.

39. *Braised potato and chicken*
Affects: stomach, large intestines
1 chicken chopped small, 400 g/1 lb potatoes sliced, 1 onion;
add other calming or neutral vegetables to taste;
add stock or water and braise gently until done.

40. *Stewed beef and potatoes*
Affects: stomach, large intestines
400 g/1 lb beef, 200 g/8 oz potatoes;

chop and slice ingredients, adding other calming or neutral vegetables if desired;
cook in water or stock to taste, adding condiments.

41. *Chicken soup*

Affects: stomach, large intestines
1 chopped chicken, 200 g/8 oz potatoes, 1 onion, water and condiments to taste;
boil in 1·5 l/2½ pt water until reduced to 900 ml/1½ pt.

42. *Braised eggplant and fish*

Affects: stomach, intestines
200 g/8 oz eggplant (aubergine), 200 g/8 oz white fish, 25 g/1 oz garlic;
add desired condiments and small quantity of vegetable oil and water as necessary;
braise to taste.
Warning: do not eat this dish if you are a yin type or if you are suffering from a deficient condition.

43. *Fried eggplant*

Affects: stomach, intestines
Take the desired quantity of eggplants (aubergines) and slice them up;
dust them with salted cornflour and flour;
fry in vegetable oil to taste.
Warning: do not eat this dish if you are a yin type or if you are suffering from a deficient condition.

44. *Braised duck in tomato sauce*

Affects: lungs, kidneys

Take 250 g/10 oz duck chopped small, 75 g/3 oz tomato purée, raw brown sugar, one tablespoon of wine, some salt and water and any other condiments to taste;
braise gently until done, adding more water if necessary.

45. *Duck soup*
Affects: lungs, kidneys
Take 1 whole duck and chop it up, 100 g/4 oz button mushrooms, 75 g/3 oz asparagus, 100 g/4 oz sliced pork and add condiments to taste;
boil in 1·5 l/2½ pt water until reduced to 900 ml/1½ pt.

46. *Steamed crab*
Affects: liver, stomach
Take 400 g/1 lb crab, 50 g/2 oz spring onions, 50 g/2 oz crushed fresh ginger;
suspend crab over small quantity of water;
steam until done.

47. *Crab stew*
Affects: liver, stomach
Take 100 g/4 oz crab meat, 6 g/¼ oz fresh ginger, 25 g/1 oz peas, 25 g/1 oz ham, salt and condiments to taste;
boil in 600 ml/1 pt water until reduced to half.

48. *Almonds and fruit*
Affects: lungs, large intestine
Take 150 g/6 oz almond beancurd (buy in Chinese supermarket or speciality health-food

store), mix with one large tin of mixed fruit; cool in refrigerator and eat.

Note: normally we would not recommend fruit tinned in syrup but the calming quality of the beancurd balances the heating qualities of the syrup and the tinning process.

49. *Steamed beancurd*

Affects: lungs, large intestine
Take 200 g/8 oz beancurd, 25 g/1 oz spring onions, some soy sauce;
steam all gently until warm.

50. *Mixed beancurd soup*

Affects: lungs, large intestines
150 g/6 oz beancurd, 100 g/4 oz sliced pork, 50 g/2 oz button or Chinese mushrooms, plus desired flavourings and condiments;
boil in 600 ml/1 pt water until tasty.

51. *Beancurd and fish soup*

Affects: lungs, large intestine
Take 200 g/8 oz beancurd, 300 g/12 oz fish, 25 g/1 oz fresh ginger, some fresh black pepper, 2 tomatoes and other condiments to taste;
boil in 600 ml/1 pt water until done.

52. *Steamed oysters*

Affects: liver, kidneys
Take 400 g/1 lb oysters, 25 g/1 oz spring onions, small quantity of ginger juice, some salt;
steam over small quantity of water.

53. *Deep-fried oysters*
Affects: liver, kidneys
Take 200 g/8 oz oysters, cover them with a paste made from flour, salt and cornflour in water;
deep-fry in peanut or corn oil.

54. *Kelp soup*
Affects: liver, stomach
Take 75 g/3 oz kelp, 100 g/4 oz sliced beef, condiments to taste;
boil in 600 ml/1 pt water until reduced to half.

55. *Lettuce salad*
Affects: stomach, intestines
Take 400 g/1 lb lettuce, 75 g/3 oz garlic, tear up lettuce and chop garlic; make a dressing of your choice;
eat!

56. *Lettuce soup*
Affects: stomach, intestines
400 g/1 lb lettuce, 25 g/1 oz fresh ginger, 100 g/4 oz freshwater fish, 3 slices pork or beef;
chop meat, fish and vegetables, but leave lettuce whole;
add condiments to taste;
cook in 1·8 l/3 pt water until ready.

57. *White mushroom salad*
Affects: liver, stomach
Take the desired quantity of fresh button mushrooms and make the dressing of your choice;
eat!

58. *Sautéed white mushroom and chicken*
Affects: liver, stomach
Take 400 g/1 lb button mushrooms, 200 g/8 oz chopped chicken, 25 g/1 oz fresh ginger, 75 g/3 oz carrots and condiments to taste;
sauté in vegetable oil and water if necessary.

59. *Mushroom soup*
Affects: liver, stomach
Take 100 g/4 oz button mushrooms, 50 g/2 oz sliced chicken, 50 g/2 oz cream, condiments, stock or water;
boil until ready.

60. *Sautéed cucumber and duck soup*
Affects: stomach, small intestine
200 g/8 oz sliced cucumber, 150 g/6 oz duck meat, condiments to taste;
boil in 600 ml/1 pt water until reduced to half.

61. *Sautéed cucumber*
Affects: stomach, small intestine
Take 150 g/6 oz cucumber, 100 g/4 oz pineapple, 75 g/3 oz green chilli, 100 g/4 oz beef, some sugar and some vinegar (wine, cider or rice), plus condiments to taste;
sauté gently until done.

62. *Steamed beancurd*
Affects: lungs, large intestine
200 g/8 oz beancurd, 25 g/1 oz spring onions (white part only), small amount of soy sauce;
cook together over small quantity of water until warm.

63. *Beancurd soup*

Affects: lungs, large intestine
150 g/6 oz beancurd, 100 g/4 oz sliced pork, 50 g/2 oz button mushrooms, add condiments to taste;
boil in 600 ml/1 pt water to taste.

64. *Beancurd and fish soup*

Affects: lungs, large intestine
Take 200 g/8 oz beancurd, 150 g/12 oz fish, 25 g/1 oz fresh ginger or fresh black pepper, 2 tomatoes and add condiments to taste;
boil in 900 ml/1½ pt water to taste.

65. *Sautéed snail*

Affects: spleen, kidneys
Take 250 g/10 oz snails, 50 g/2 oz garlic, 12 g/½ oz fresh ginger, 75 g/3 oz red chilli, 6 g/¼ oz mustard, some salt and soy sauce;
sauté in small quantity of vegetable oil.

66. *Baked snail*

Affects: spleen, kidneys
Take 250 g/10 oz snails, 100 g/4 oz onion, 50 g/2 oz garlic, some soy sauce and butter;
put into small earthenware pot and bake in oven or over direct heat.

67. *Tomato salad*

Affects: liver, spleen, stomach
Take as many tomatoes as you want, make a dressing of your choice;
eat!

68. *Mixed tomato soup*

Affects: liver, spleen, stomach
Take 100 g/4 oz tomatoes, 2 onions, 50 g/2 oz garlic, 100 g/4 oz celery, 50 g/2 oz chopped pork, 75 g/3 oz carrot;
chop and slice all ingredients and add desired condiments;
boil in 900 ml/1½ pt water until ready.

69. *Sautéed peas*

Affects: heart, spleen, stomach, large intestine
Take 100 g/4 oz peas, 75 g/3 oz sliced chicken, 12 g/½ oz garlic, 1 onion and add necessary condiments;
sauté all together in small quantity of vegetable oil, plus water if desired.

70. *Pea soup*

Affects: heart, spleen, stomach, large intestine
Take 75 g/3 oz peas, 50 g/2 oz chicken, 50 g/2 oz fresh cream, 1 onion;
add condiments and boil in 600 ml/1 pt water until ready.

71. *Spinach*

Affects: large and small intestines, stomach and bladder
Take 400 g/1 lb spinach, 37 g/1½ oz garlic;
cook gently with very small quantity of water.

72. *Spinach soup*

Affects: large and small intestines, stomach and bladder
Take 400 g/1 lb spinach, 25 g/1 oz sliced beef,

125 g/5 oz beancurd, plus condiments as desired;
add water and make into soup, to taste.

Neutral recipes

73. *Sautéed cabbage and pork*
Affects: stomach
Take 400 g/1 lb cabbage, 150 g/6 oz sliced pork, 50 g/2 oz bacon;
add condiments to taste and sauté in small amount of vegetable oil, adding water if desired.

74. *Cabbage soup*
Affects: stomach
200 g/8 oz cabbage, 150 g/6 oz beef, 100 g/4 oz carrots, 100 g/4 oz celery, 2 onions;
slice and chop everything, add condiments;
cook in water and stock, to taste.

75. *Braised black mushrooms and chicken*
Affects: liver
Take 150 g/6 oz black mushrooms (dried Chinese), 200 g/8 oz sliced chicken, 25 g/1 oz fresh ginger, plus condiments to taste;
braise in small amount of vegetable oil, adding water or stock if desired.

76. *Black mushroom soup*
Affects: liver
Take 100 g/4 oz Chinese dried black mushrooms, 200 g/8 oz sliced chicken and add any condiments desired;
boil in water or stock until ready.

77. *French beans and pork*

Affects: spleen, stomach
150 g/6 oz French beans, 100 g/4 oz sliced pork, 12 g/½ oz fresh garlic, add condiments to taste;
sauté in small amount of vegetable oil, adding some water if necessary.

78. *Steamed abalone*

Affects: liver, lungs
Take 250 g/10 oz abalone, sliced very finely, 25 g/1 oz spring onions, soy sauce, salt and other desired condiments;
steam over small quantity of water.

79. *Braised taro and duck*

Affects: spleen, stomach
Take 200 g/8 oz taro, 200 g/8 oz duck, chop up both and add condiments to taste;
braise in small amount of vegetable oil.

80. *Fried taro cakes*

Affects: spleen, stomach
Blend 200 g/8 oz taro, adding some flour, ½ teaspoonful of salt and some small pieces of bacon;
shape into little cakes and deep-fry in corn or peanut oil.

81. *Roast quail*

Affects: lungs, spleen
Dip plucked quails in a mixture of soy sauce, sugar, wine and ginger juice;
coat the skin with honey and roast.

82. *Quail soup*
Affects: lungs, spleen
Take 4 or 5 quails, 125 ml/5 fl oz coconut juice, 75 g/3 oz pork, 600 ml/1 pt water;
add other necessary condiments;
boil for 2 or 3 hours, to taste.

83. *Catfish and garlic*
Affects: spleen, kidneys
Take 300 g/12 oz catfish, 50 g/2 oz garlic, some salt and soy sauce;
braise in small amount of vegetable oil, adding water if necessary.

84. *Braised pork and vegetables*
Affects: spleen, kidneys
250 g/10 oz pork, 50 g/2 oz tomatoes, 2 slices fresh ginger, garlic, spring onions, soy sauce, raw brown sugar;
braise in small amount of vegetable oil, adding water if necessary.

85. *Pork and vegetable soup*
Affects: spleen, kidneys
Take 200 g/8 oz pork, 100 g/4 oz potatoes, 75 g/3 oz tomatoes, 25 g/1 oz garlic, 75 g/3 oz onion salt, soy sauce to taste;
boil in water until ready.

86. *Beef and cauliflower*
Affects: stomach, spleen
Take 400 g/1 lb cauliflower, 150 g/6 oz sliced beef, 25 g/1 oz garlic, plus other condiments if desired;

sauté all together in small amount of vegetable oil.

87. *Honey chicken*

Affects: lungs, spleen, large intestine
Take 600 g/1½ lb chopped chicken, 300 g/12 oz honey, 100 g/4 oz sliced ginger, some vegetable oil;
braise gently, adding liquid if necessary.

88. *Sautéed clams*

Affects: lungs, liver, spleen
100 g/4 oz clams, 75 g/3 oz green chilli, 75 g/3 oz onions, some raw brown sugar, soy sauce;
sauté in a little peanut oil.

89. *Braised garlic eel*

Affects: spleen, lungs, kidneys
400 g/1 lb saltwater eel, 75 g/3 oz garlic, 25 g/1 oz fresh ginger, 25 g/1 oz spring onions, some salt, soy sauce and vegetable oil;
braise gently, adding liquid if necessary.

90. *Eel soup*

Affects: spleen, lungs, kidneys
400 g/1 lb freshwater eel, 100 g/½ oz fresh black pepper, salt;
boil in 1·8 l/3 pt water until reduced by half.

91. *Fried perch fingers*

Affects: spleen, stomach, liver, kidneys
Take 250 g/10 oz fish and make into fingers,

cover each with cornflour, egg white, salt and flour;
deep-fry in peanut oil.

92. *Sesame porridge*

Affects: lungs, spleen, large intestine, kidneys
Take 200 g/8 oz powdered black sesame seeds, 100 g/4 oz raw brown sugar and 150 ml/6 fl oz milk and stir together with some water;
boil until cooked, stirring continually.

Bibliography

We cannot suggest a very extensive reading list in this subject for the reason that almost all the relevant books exist only in the original Chinese. However, the short list below will help to extend your knowledge further.

Chang, K. C. (ed.), *Food in Chinese Culture*, Yale University Press, USA, 1977

Horwitz, Ted and Kimmelman, Susan with Lui, H.H., *Tai Chi Chu'an: The Technique of Power*, Rider, London, 1979

Kaptchuk, Ted J., *Chinese Medicine: The Web that Has No Weaver*, Rider, London, 1983

Ko Hung, *Alchemy, Medicine and Religion in the China of AD320: The Nei P'ien of Ko Hung*, Massachusetts Institute of Technology, USA, 1966

Koo, Linda chih-ling, *Nourishment of Life: Health in Chinese Society*, Commercial Press, Hong Kong

Veith, Ilza (trans.), *The Yellow Emperor's Classic of Internal Medicine*, U.Cal.Press, 1972

Index

On the following pages are details of Arrow books that will be of interest.

THE BOOK OF CHINESE BELIEFS

Frena Bloomfield

Earth magic, ghost weddings, passports to the after-life: the spirit world of the Chinese exists side-by-side with everyday reality, and affects every aspect of Chinese life from diet and decor to getting married or opening a business.

Frena Bloomfield has lived and worked in Hong Kong and has talked in depth to many practitioners of the magic arts. *The Book of Chinese Beliefs* is a fascinating introduction to a rich culture where the dead are ever-present and even the siting of a house or village is governed by the laws of earth magic.

NO CHANGE

A biological revolution
for women

Wendy Cooper

For years, women approaching middle age have been told by their doctors, 'It's just your age, you must put up with it.' Now they don't have to put up with it, there is a choice.

Wendy Cooper describes how modern medicine can offer many women the chance to minimize the effects of the menopause, now recognized as a hormone deficiency condition.

'A heartening, encouraging contribution to the subject.'

Sunday Telegraph

'A book which could alter the life of every woman in the 40–60 age group.'

Woman

BABYSHOCK

Dr John Cobb

'I just don't think you have any idea of what motherhood is like until it happens . . .'

An authoritative, sympathetic guide to see the new mother through the first five years, BABYSHOCK is the first book of its kind to consider in depth the emotional, physical and practical problems that may concern a woman both during pregnancy and after the birth. Fully updated for this paperback edition, it helps to answer the many questions new mothers ask about, everything from emotional tension and stress to babysitters, state benefits and returning to work.

A unique survival guide, reference source and companion through the early crises of motherhood, BABYSHOCK can help to make this demanding time as rewarding and fulfilling as it is often difficult.

'Excellent' *Nursing Mirror*

'Endlessly helpful' Catherine Stott, *Sunday Telegraph*

YOUR PSYCHIC WORLD A-Z
An everyday guide

Ann Petrie

Everyone is psychic.

Everyone has the ability to develop extrasensory perception, but few know what to do with it.

Taking examples from everyday life, this book looks at the efficiency of your energy and your love, and presents a whole new perspective on the psychic world.

It explains *why* certain unusual or uncanny situations occur, and how to handle them in ways most beneficial to you and those around you.

This guide tells you what to do if you — Meet a ghost, a ghoul or a poltergeist; Feel you've been cursed; Fall in love at first sight; Remember places you know you've never been to before; Have dreams that come true; Need to protect yourself from psychic attack — plus many more pieces of essential advice on relating to the psychic world around you.

Ann Petrie is a psychic-astrologer who combines her gifts in a unique way in writing, broadcasting and counselling.